METAMORPHOSIS

UNLOCKING YOUR SPIRITUAL TRANSFORMATION THROUGH HEALTHY DISCIPLESHIP

MATT HATCH

SEQUOIA TREE BOOKS

Published by Sequioa Tree Books 2023

ISBN: 978-1-7384088-0-1

e-ISBN: 978-1-7384088-1-8

CONTENTS

ACKNOWLEDGEMENTS

This book has emerged from countless hours spent with some incredible people and joining them on their discipleship journey. I always seem to learn something from seeing God at work in their lives. I'm grateful for them and for Mosaic Church giving me space and time to learn how to guide people to Jesus and the transformation he promises.

I'm indebted to Ian Galloway, Ralph Buckingham and Daniel McGinnis for encouraging me to start my book-writing adventure and giving helpful insights that have made this a better book.

In particular, I'm thankful for Adam Sewell, Steve Haines, Jeff Bailey, and Simon Holley, who gave hours and hours to reading the manuscript and giving detailed feedback. I'm also grateful to Abi Flavell for her prophetic encouragement that got this book started in the first place and her advice on how to structure each chapter. I also want to thank Jane Sanders for her skill in helping a preacher become a writer. The book is so much better for her hard work behind the scenes. Lastly, I want to thank my wife, Philippa for her love, example and passion for integrity.

To protect the privacy of those I've discipled, every person's story I've shared has been altered in some way and their names have been changed. Notably, despite these amendments, they are real people who have embraced real discipleship and who have experienced real transformation.

RECOMMENDATIONS

"*Metamorphosis* is exactly the book that I want to give to a long list of people — young adults just getting started in life, seasoned Christians wanting to go deeper, and spiritual seekers exploring a path to faith. The book brims with humour, kindness, and authenticity. It offers a wise, relational, and intensely practical path towards genuine life change. I can't recommend it highly enough."

Rev'd Canon Jeff Bailey, PhD
Canon for Leadership Development, Anglican Church in North America

"Thank you, Matt, for writing this book about the life we all long for. As disciples of Jesus, we're called to live in the freedom Christ has provided for us and also to impart that to others in fulfilling our destiny. *Metamorphosis* is modelled in Matt's personal life and is an invitation for all of us to go and do the same."

Jimmy Seibert
Founder and Senior Pastor of Antioch Church, Waco

"Having been part of a church led by Matt I have experienced first-hand his passion for discipleship. This book unpacks years of his own journey of learning to be more like Jesus and his experience of helping others do the same. Matt gives vision for doing the hard work of discipleship, shares authentically about his own journey of sanctification and outlines tools that anyone can use to grow in their relationship with God. As followers of Jesus our primary goal should be to become more and more like Him - this is the privilege of discipleship. *Metamorphosis* will be a great help to you as you pursue this journey; as you look to be transformed from the inside out."

Wendy Mann
Author of 'Naturally Supernatural'

"I have learned so much about discipleship, Christian habits and spiritual growth from Matt Hatch. I am so pleased that he has shared his wisdom and his story in this short, accessible book."

Andrew Wilson, PhD
Teaching Pastor at King's Church, London and author of 'Remaking the World: How 1776 Created the Post-Christian West.'

"I am so pleased that my friend, Matt Hatch has written this book. Matt has a good track record in developing disciples and training leaders. The book focuses on our inner life which is so important for growing in godly character and training in righteousness. I am pleased to commend *Metamorphosis* to all who seek to make disciples as Jesus commanded and to continue to grow in godliness themselves."

David Devenish
Author of 'Fathering Leaders, Motivating Mission'.

"This book is all about change and how it happens. Change is essential for discipleship, and this book makes it real and practical for everyone."

Steve Nicholson
Founding pastor of Vineyard Christian Church of Evanston

"Matt has spent years doing what he is writing about. He shares the victories and failures with the utmost candour and consequently enables the rest of us to accelerate our learning and become that much more effective at the essential task of making disciples."

David Stroud
Senior Leader, Christ Church London, co-Founder, The Everything
Conference

Matt Hatch has been passionate about making disciples for as long as I've known him. He lays out such a clear process in this book condensing years of experience into simple to follow concepts that will enable anyone to become more like Jesus themselves and then go on to help others do the same. It's not just another evangelistic tool or model. It's a framework to create healthy, well-rounded disciples that bring life and change to the world around them as they themselves are transformed by Christ. Don't hesitate to buy it!

Simon Holley
Leader of Catalyst Family of Churches

"I've known Matt Hatch for many years now, and I'm delighted that he's written this important book about Christian discipleship. What I appreciate most about him is that he lives what he teaches and everything he writes comes from his experience. *Metamorphosis* is not a book for the faint of heart or for those who want to live comfortably. It is just the right balance of vulnerability and challenge and of inspiration and practicality. In my own life, spiritual and personal growth has been my constant hope, and I appreciate how Matt is honest about how hard it can be to hold onto this without growing disillusioned and yet still holds firmly to the priority of growth in all areas of our lives.

After starting with key foundations and attitudes of Christian discipleship in Part One, including the hallmarks of surrender, encounter, and obedience, Part Two unveils a unique framework for how personal transformation actually happens in the believer's life. This is the highlight of the book and is a memorable set of ways to conceptualise this vital lifelong process, including story-based tools and the change circle. Part Three then walks through crucial discipleship rhythms and practices, following a classic up, in, out pattern.

Throughout there are practical suggestions and relatable personal stories, along with helpful questions for reflection at the end of each chapter. It is not always feel-good or comfortable reading because it seeks to take its readers beyond their comfort zone into authentic spiritual formation, but it is joyful and hopeful throughout. If your desire is to walk more deeply with Jesus, be radically transformed in his presence, and live a fruitful missional life that impacts others, then this is the book for you."

Dr. Daniel McGinnis, PhD
Principal, St Hild College

"I'm so excited by Matt Hatch's new book *Metamorphosis*. For many years Matt Hatch has been one of the leading voices in the UK on the conversation of intentional discipleship to Jesus. His church Mosaic has been built around the principles you'll read in this book, and it is a church alive in the Spirit with a holistic vision of spiritual formation and a proven track record of seeing people come to faith, come alive in faith, and journey towards Christlikeness. This book is an incredible opportunity to learn from Matt, Mosaic, and the journey they have been on."

Pete Hughes, Leader of KXC, London

For free discipleship resources and downloads, visit
www.matthatch.org

This includes an exclusive training video -
*'Three things holding back your transformation and
what you can do about them'*, downloadable PDFs,
and a 'How to start a Triplet' manual.

PART 1

WHAT HEALTHY DISCIPLESHIP LOOKS LIKE

SEQUOIA TREE BOOKS

"There is no problem in human life that apprenticeship to Jesus cannot solve."

Dallas Willard
(quoted in John Ortberg, Eternity is now in session)

ONE

WHY I WROTE THIS BOOK

Sometimes in life, you get a window into your soul, a seemingly trivial moment that reveals something more profound. For me, it happened as I was cooking a curry for our new church planting team. As I began to prepare the food, the handle broke on my wok. Quickly I grabbed my two young children and set off to the nearest grocery store to buy a new one. I put the kids in the shopping trolley, picked out the wok and made my way to the cashier.

To our amazement, as I handed it over to be scanned, the wok had miraculously filled with water, which was swishing about inside it. The cashier and I looked at the mysterious liquid, then at each other, and then back at the wok.

We were utterly perplexed. Where on earth had it come from? Was there a leak in the roof? Had something spilt into it? With horror, we both turned to my children (aged three and one) and realised that it must have come from them. I led the investigation and found I'd forgotten to put a nappy on my youngest child, who had urinated directly into the wok. And now I stood before a cashier with a wok full of wee. I was embarrassed. The cashier was flustered. The kids were completely oblivious to the chaos they had created. Even the supervisor was at a loss to know what to do. We eventually found some paper towels and tried to soak up the worst of it.

Later that day, we had our church planting team over for dinner. They were all wonderful people we had met in Leeds, and we were dreaming of starting a church together. None of them was fully committed - everyone was still checking us out. We were hoping they'd like us and stick around. Midway through the curry, I remembered my hilarious incident at the grocery store and told the story. I was approaching my entertaining punchline when it dawned on me that I had cooked the curry in the wok my child had filled with wee. And worse, after getting distracted dealing with the kids, I had never washed the wok.

As my story ended, I knew I was facing a *discipleship moment*. Would I act with integrity, confess my unfortunate mistake and set an example of honesty? I wish the answer were yes, but in fact I said nothing. A quick mental cost/benefit analysis meant that I decided to keep silent and ignore the quiet inner voice encouraging me to own up and apologise. I enjoyed my friends' laughter, but inwardly I knew I should interrupt the hilarity and tell the truth. It may seem a small thing, but it revealed a tendency in me to cover things up or tell 'little white lies' for my own benefit. And I knew this wouldn't be the end of the story.

The next day, my misstep was an opportunity for God to gently reveal his love and invite me to be honest with him. You'll be glad to hear I eventually confessed to my team, and they were very gracious and chose to forgive me - even if their stomachs churned at the thought of eating food cooked in the remnants of my child's wee. Moments like these, when God graciously gives us opportunity to recognise and change our wrong attitudes and behaviour, are what I call *discipleship moments*, and they can be transformational in our lives.

We long for Transformation

Deep down, I think we all long for transformation in the small and the big things. Despite our failures and backward steps, most of us want to be more like Jesus. We desperately want to respond obediently in these sorts of *discipleship moments*. We yearn for change, and when it doesn't come immediately, it's easy to feel despondent and defeated.

We know our lives are both magnificent and messy. Some days I'm celebrating the ways God's grace has led me to experience a massive transformation in my thinking and behaviour; on other days I feel I've gone backwards. There are moments when the last thing I want to do is be loving, patient, humble, or sacrificial, and other moments when those qualities seem to flow easily from my heart. Sometimes I can feel both weak and broken but, at the same time, confident and secure. I can be aware of the crushing weight of my sinfulness and the lightness of unlimited grace and acceptance.

The remarkable reality is that God remains faithfully committed to helping me become more like Jesus, in spite of all my failures and inconsistency. Even more remarkably, God loves using messy people (like me) to lead other messy people (like you) towards his Son, Jesus and into his mission. This beautiful, grace-filled process is called **discipleship**.

If you're a Christian, you're already a disciple, chosen by Jesus to be with him, live life for him, become like him, and share in his mission to see the earth filled with the knowledge of his glory. This comes from the very heart of God, who intends to complete the work he's started in us. As Paul wrote to the Christians in Philippi, *'being confident of this, that he who began a good work in you will carry it on to completion until the day of Christ Jesus.'* (Philippians 1:6). The Greek verb *'to carry on to completion'* is written in the future tense which means God will be at work today, tomorrow and the day after that until he has finished the good work of transformation.

When Discipleship disappoints

Discipleship, the process of following Jesus, should be a joyful, life-giving path into mission and maturity, but that may not always have been our experience. Our discipleship journey may have been non-existent or unhelpful. The person doing the discipling may have been overbearing and controlling or focused on modifying external behaviour, rather than addressing an inward change of thinking and attitudes. We may feel that the way we've been taught to live as Christians hasn't led to the transformed life we longed for and expected.

Perhaps Christlikeness was made to look dull and lifeless. Or perhaps we've had a negative view of ourselves as undisciplined, poorly motivated and unable to embrace habits that would help us become more like Jesus.

My own worst discipleship experience was, ironically, working as a carpenter in Bethlehem! I had just left school and decided to spend three months walking closely in Jesus' footsteps, and my job was to help an experienced carpenter make and mend things in a Bible college. It might sound like a great adventure and wonderful learning experience, but in fact it was anything but.

I wasn't ever shown *how* to fix the timber to the wall, *how* to measure, cut and create a joint. My jobs were uncomplicated and uninvolved: hold this; carry that; lift that a fraction; put your weight on that end. I was never shown *why* or *how*. At times I had no idea what we were even building. I spent hour upon hour watching but never doing. At no point did I feel I could join in. I simply made up the numbers and contributed hardly anything. It felt unfulfilling and pointless.

There came a moment when I was finally given a proper task, of putting up some shelves. It was a simple job, but I failed miserably. Even though I hadn't been shown how to do it, my failure was met with exasperation - and I wasn't asked to do anything else. What's disappointing is that it could have been so much better. I could easily have been mentored, shown how to do the work and then released to do it myself, and who knows, maybe I'd have reached the point of being able to train someone else to do what I'd learnt!

It's possible for Christians to feel a similar sense of frustration and disappointment when it comes to discipleship. We want to follow Jesus well, but it may be that we haven't been shown *how*, and since we don't know what to do, we end up doing nothing. Or perhaps there was a time when we focused on being disciples and discipling others, but it didn't go to plan, our high expectations weren't realised, and we were left disappointed. Others of us may feel tired and worn down by seemingly fruitless efforts to disciple ourselves and others.

Some of us may be disappointed that we haven't seen more transformation of our character and lifestyle since becoming a Christian. We may have run out of steam in terms of maintaining a relationship with Jesus through worship, prayer and reading the Bible. Maybe we hoped a spiritual "silver bullet" would rid us of the junk in our lives, but we found that habitual sin or addiction returned, or morphed into something else. Maybe we got exhausted. Maybe the insecurities in our hearts were never dealt with. Or maybe it just seems too frightening to take a deep, honest look into our own hearts and hurts. Perhaps we started well, but have lost momentum and find ourselves in a place of compromise and disobedience. Whatever the cause, we've somehow plateaued. We're not changing. We're godly enough to get by, but the reality is that our vision for being transformed has faded.

What can make it feel worse is that we've probably tried really hard to mature. We haven't sat around doing nothing, but have given ourselves afresh to God time after time. We may have given our all to stop doing certain things that lead us away from Jesus and tried to start other things to draw us closer to him. Maybe we've made New Year's resolutions or tried over Lent to overcome habitual sin or spend time every day with Jesus. But after a few days we've found that we didn't keep to what we'd set out to do, and we got discouraged and found ourselves back at square one.

Maybe we're afraid that we can never give enough or do enough to really please God, and so we see ourselves as spiritual failures. We can end up being so hard on ourselves that we lose hope in God's power to bring change in our lives and our ability to obey his commands.

At such moments, it's easy to hate ourselves and feel miserable, embarrassed at how immature we seem to be. We know we're forgiven and will spend eternity with God, we're assured that he loves us but we're not sure if he *likes* us.

It might be that the vision for maturity has been over-promised and un-der-delivered, so that we're in danger of becoming cynical about the whole process. We no longer believe that the day to day experience of relationship with God can be full of freedom, joy and delight.

Discipleship - God's best for us

Yet, having described our collective sense of disappointment, fatigue, apathy and underperformance, I want to call us back to the hope of transformational discipleship. I believe God has much more for us as individuals and as churches, and that God has given us everything we need for life and godliness.[1]

Spiritual growth and transformation aren't just something we're 'supposed' to engage in if we're Christians - they're God's *best* for us. At its heart, being a Christian is about being with Jesus, letting him loose in our lives to help us become the people he created us to be, and then following him into the world he loves to share his Good News and partner with him in growing his kingdom on earth. This is what we were created for - the life we were created to *enjoy*.

Is it all enjoyment? No. It will involve dying to our old lives and taking up the new life Jesus offers, and at times this may be costly. But it will involve sitting at the feet of the greatest teacher ever to have walked our planet, listening to his words and obeying them. Our discipleship journey leads us into a deeper and deeper union with Jesus as we worship him, receive him, follow him, become his friends and increasingly become like him, joining his mission and helping others to do the same. In other words, all healthy discipleship has Jesus at its epicentre, and that's good news.

Also, Jesus calls his disciples into a radical freedom. This freedom is to love God wholeheartedly and grow to love others without the influence of selfishness, greed, lies and desire. Discipleship to Jesus offers the possibility of freedom from guilt and shame. It means the past doesn't have to define our future and the sins committed against us don't have to keep us in bondage. We gain freedom to extend forgiveness and mercy as we receive forgiveness and mercy from God. Discipleship offers us a way through the crushing weight of anxiety and the gravitational pull of consumerism by drawing our gaze towards Jesus. In discipleship we are freed to be the people God created us to be.

I've spent my life slowly learning, with others, how God loves to lead his church towards healthy, transformational, multiplying disciple-making, and I'd love to share with you the lessons he's taught me.

I am utterly convinced that discipleship is life-giving, powerful and ultimately joyful and satisfying beyond measure. But we will need to make some radical changes and do some things differently. Albert Einstein once said that the definition of insanity is doing the same thing over and over and expecting to get a different result! So this book will invite us to engage with some new ways of thinking and to change some of our habits in line with what the Bible teaches, so that we can begin to experience the transformed lives we long for.

What to expect?

Transformative discipleship is not just for "leaders" – it's for *every* follower of Jesus. It's freely available, but at the same time, it's supremely costly. It's about letting go of things we've previously considered precious and important, in order to gain Jesus, and then helping others to do the same. It's not about simply adding Jesus to our current list of precious things, rather, it's about exchanging them and their priority in our lives, in order to gain Christ and become his apprentice.[2]

We live in a world of instant gratification and instant results. I wish there were a similarly quick and painless route to transforming our lives, but the reality is that a process of self-denial is part of God's programme of maturity. Jesus said, *'Whoever wants to be my disciple must deny themselves and take up their cross and follow me.'* (Matthew 16:24)

Therefore, this book may not be an easy read in some places. I hope to challenge us to pursue transformational disciple-making in the strongest possible terms, and with myself as a fellow learner. I will endeavour to be honest and open about what discipleship looks like in my life. This will make me a bit uncomfortable at some points, but I hope it will help you see the practical and emotional dimensions of change. I don't particularly want you to know how immature I can be, and where I still struggle, but I hope that sharing my weaknesses will give you permission to be honest about your own.

Transformation can be yours

This book is packed with fresh hope and passion for disciple-making. A few years ago, one of our leaders at Mosaic ran a discipleship group which included a young man who had struggled all his life with shame and the fear of rejection. He bravely explained how a family member would humiliate him by urinating into his bed at night and forcing him to watch porn. Unsurprisingly, he was bound by anxiety and shame. While the internal struggles left him exhausted, he had developed ways of coping on the outside by avoiding certain social settings, hiding his true personality in public, and never drawing attention to himself. This internal struggle left him exhausted. At the same time, though, he also felt God calling him to evangelism and sharing his faith.

With the support of the discipleship group, he gradually began to believe that Jesus could set him free from fear and shame, beyond anything he'd imagined possible. He started to recognise the coping mechanisms he had put in place to help him get through life, and by finding a safe space to talk about the shameful acts committed against him, he began to receive the love and forgiveness of God. He realised that he could become the man God had created him to be by embracing his true identity in Christ and walking through his fear into freedom. He surrendered his desire to hide and pretend, in order to radically live for God. He adopted certain habits to help him grow in intimacy with God, and experienced breakthrough in sharing with his friends when before, he had given into fear. He even managed to begin the process of forgiving the family member who had abused him.

This young man is now a completely different person. He makes a daily choice to die to his old life of fear and embrace his new life in Christ, and is now a fantastic evangelist who has led many people to Christ. His story inspires many others who struggle to overcome their shame, fear and anxiety, and his story of inner transformation could be your story, too. The details of your life are, of course, different, but the power of God to bring healing, freedom and change is as available to you as to him.

What are we here for?

This book is written from my experience of leading two churches into disciple-making over the last 25 years, particularly Mosaic Church in Leeds. When we started Mosaic in 2004, we were given many different scriptures and images that shaped our vision. Much of the prophetic imagery used to describe the church was about boats (which is somewhat ironic, since Leeds is nearly the furthest point from the sea in the UK): boats being built and designed; crew being trained; champagne being smashed over the bow as the ship is launched; sails being raised. And over time, three distinct, repeated pictures emerged that helped us understand the kind of church God was calling us to build.

First, we're called to sail in a ship called 'Mosaic' that helps people follow Jesus, build community and make disciples locally and globally. We want to see everyone experience the transforming power of the gospel and be trained to help others do the same.

Second, we're also called to be a shipyard—a place where other boats are built. We're to multiply disciples, leaders, sites and churches.

Lastly, we're to be part of an armada, a fearsome, kingdom-fighting force made up of lots of different boats. We're not to do this alone, but instead sail alongside many other churches to play our part in the Great Commission Jesus gave us, to make disciples of all nations.

This book invites you to draw your boat alongside us so that we can learn and grow together. It aims to help anyone who feels that they have plateaued spiritually or who is looking for the next steps in their discipleship journey. It seeks to offer fresh hope for growth and maturity, and provide practical tools along the way.

How the book is structured

We will begin in Part One by examining the biblical hallmarks of healthy discipleship, the key characteristics and attitudes that will help us experience transformation and give us confidence to move forward in our journey with Jesus.

In Part Two we will explore how God actually changes us from within. The more we understand this process, the easier it is to cooperate with him. I'll present key discipleship principles that unlock situations where we may feel spiritually stuck. We'll also look at simple tools to help us understand *what* we should do to experience transformation.

Part Three identifies the most important activities, rhythms and practices that open us to the transformation process, and explains how engaging with these can help us embrace *discipleship moments* as they occur.

Each chapter will end with questions to help you process your thoughts and actions. As you read, I'd encourage you to take some time to allow God to speak to you about the implications for your life and how He wants you to respond.

Questions

1. How do you feel about the discipleship you've experienced in your own life? What has worked well and why? What was unhelpful?

2. Are you full of hope regarding your growth and maturity? If so, what are your expectations of how that will happen? Or have you plateaued in your discipleship journey? What happened? Can you relate to feeling weary or cynical about growth?

3. Consider how your church disciples people - what is emphasised or modelled? What is the expectation for people to become disciples who make disciples?

4. What are some key discipleship moments in your life, and what did you learn from them? Moreover, have you experienced God transforming and healing these broken and painful parts of your life or is there more work to be done?

---

1. 2 Peter 1:3

2. Matthew 13:44-46

"Be with Jesus. Become like him. Do as he did."

John Mark Comer
(Practicing the Way)

TWO

DISCIPLESHIP BASICS

S ometimes you can watch a film that leaves an indelible mark on your soul. For me, it was Steven Spielberg's epic Second World War film *'Saving Private Ryan.'* My kids tell me it's a really old film now, but it feels like I first watched it yesterday. When it was first released, D-Day veterans commended its true-to-life depiction of the landing of American soldiers on Omaha Beach in France, and the film changed the way battle scenes have been depicted on the big screen ever since.

The film begins and ends with an elderly Private Ryan weeping in a Normandy graveyard, looking back at his life. He had been chosen to be evacuated from the war in France after his three brothers had died in combat. As the film unfolds, we find that almost every soldier sent on this mission to save him dies. At the gravestone of Captain Miller (played by Tom Hanks), who led the mission to save him, Ryan reflects on the captain's final words to him. Miller whispers to Ryan, *"Earn this."* He tells him, in other words, "Live a life worthy of how much this cost." In the closing scene, Private Ryan stands at the Captain's grave, asking his family, *"Have I lived a good life? Have I lived a life worthy?"*

It's a question we live with too. The Apostle Paul addresses this theme in several of his letters: *'As a prisoner for the Lord, then, I urge you to live a life worthy of the calling you have received'* (Ephesians 4:1) *'Whatever happens, conduct yourselves in a manner worthy of the gospel of Christ.'* (Philippians 1:27) We're not called to live any old life, but a life worthy of the Lord.

Radical Change

The New Testament makes it clear that it's possible for every believer to experience radical change and be able to live a transformed life, and it describes the process as having three distinct aspects. First, there is an immediate change that takes place the moment someone puts their faith in Jesus; this is *justification*. Second, there is a future transformation that will make us ready for the new creation; this is *glorification*. And third, there is a present, ongoing process of growth in Christlikeness throughout our Christian lives; this is *sanctification*. Let's look at these three in more detail.

We *have* been changed (Justification)

The Apostle Paul is brutally honest in describing the change in the Corinthians by comparing their lives before and after becoming Christians. He says that some of us were immoral, idolaters, greedy, slanderers, drunkards and swindlers but now we've been washed, sanctified and justified.[1] The transformation was spectacular -the *'unrighteous'* have been cleansed, and their identity has completely changed.

Paul explains the impact of our union with Christ as a *'death to life'* experience.[2] We have been transferred from one state to another. Our hearts are regenerated and renewed. We have been forgiven and made acceptable to God through Christ—no longer sinners but saints. The image of God has been restored in us.

Justification for the Christian leads to our adoption, redemption and reconciliation. This means our identity, family, and name are transformed. The Apostle John revelled in this new status. He says we have been born of God and we are his children. In him, we have overcome the world. Furthermore, we are now empowered to love and live differently in the world.[3] Just as those first disciples experienced, every new believer is radically empowered to love and be loved the moment they put their faith in Jesus.

We *will* be changed (Glorification)

As well as the instantaneous change from "guilty sinner" to "righteous saint" that takes place when we first put our faith in Jesus, there is a final, ultimate, instantaneous transformation that comes at the end of our lives: a glorious resurrection. Paul explains that we will be given a new, imperishable, spiritual body - *'What is sown is perishable; what is raised is imperishable. It is sown in dishonour; it is raised in glory. It is sown in weakness; it is raised in power. It is sown a natural body; it is raised a spiritual body. If there is a natural body, there is also a spiritual body.'* (1 Corinthians 15:42–44) In the new creation our sinful, corrupt and fickle hearts are fully left behind, as we step into the fulness of all that Jesus obtained for us through the cross. The transformation is complete, as all the old has gone, and the new has come completely and instantaneously: *'For the trumpet will sound, and the dead will be raised imperishable, and we shall be changed.'* (1 Corinthians 15:52)

We are *being* changed (Sanctification)

Right now, we live between these two transformations—in the season of 'the now and the not yet'. The first transformation, our entrance into God's kingdom, with our identity, standing, and relationship to God being made new in Christ has already taken place the moment we put our trust in Jesus.

The final transformation is our exit from this world into the new creation, where we will receive our resurrection bodies and be prepared for an eternity with God.

The life we now live is in the middle part, the in-between period, where we are gradually being transformed into the likeness of Jesus. As the Apostle Paul declares, *'And we know that for those who love God all things work together for good, for those who are called according to his purpose. For those whom he foreknew he also predestined to be conformed to the image of his Son, in order that he might be the firstborn among many brothers.'* (Romans 8:28-29) In other words, the "good" for which God works all things together in the lives of those who love him is the "good" of being changed to be like Jesus, and Paul encourages us that this growth to Christlike maturity is not just for a few "specially gifted" Christians, but for every believer. His desire is to present everyone mature in Christ.[4] Transformation is about becoming the people we already are in Christ. We will look at this more thoroughly in Chapter 6.

This process of ongoing transformation, or sanctification, involves us dedicating our lives to God's original plan, the plan he revealed to Adam and Eve, of expanding his kingdom across the earth through us, his image-bearers. We pursue transformation in our own lives in order to be a provocative witness in the world; we live '*in Christ*', filled with his Spirit, overcoming sin, embracing spiritual disciplines and participating with others in God's mission. You could say the gospel advances on two frontiers at the same time: to the uttermost parts of the earth and to the innermost parts of the heart. The closer we grow to God, the closer we come to fulfilling his purpose for us.

Union with Christ

This is such good news. It means whatever our background or progress in discipleship thus far, we find ourselves in the perfect place for change. Whether we are just starting out or have made many attempts to grow as a Christian, Jesus has chosen and empowered each one of us to be his disciple, and he is overjoyed to be partnering with us in our discipleship journey. We belong to him, and he will not fail us. We're already his disciples, already on the adventure of learning from him, becoming like him and partnering with him in his mission.

So how do we do it? How do we live in this 'now and not yet' season of gradual transformation? English theologian and pastor John Stott asked a similar question, 'What does it mean to become a mature disciple?' and gave a sumptuous answer: '*You'll know I'm sure that the commonest definition given anywhere in the writings of the Apostle Paul is that a Christian is a man or woman in Christ - not inside Christ, as our tools are in a box or our clothes are in a wardrobe, but united to Christ as the branches are in the vine and the vine is in the branches, or as the limbs are in the body, organically, vitally united to the body, Jesus Christ.*"[5]

Discipleship, then, is a journey into fully embracing our union with Christ. We worship Jesus, follow Jesus, receive Jesus, become friends of Jesus – and from this union we start to imitate Jesus.

The Holy Spirit - the ultimate discipler

Let's estimate that the disciples spent around eight hours a day with Jesus. Over three years, that amounts to eight thousand hours! And yet, even then, they persisted in doubt and immaturity. What hope, then, is there for us? How can we be expected to grow in maturity and holiness when it was such a struggle for those who actually walked with Jesus in human form and were discipled by him on a daily basis?

God's answer is the abiding Holy Spirit. Jesus promised his disciples that he wouldn't leave them like orphans, but would send the Holy Spirit to live in them, guide them, teach and empower them.[6] The Spirit comes to continually fill disciples with God's love and power to live impossible lives of holiness for the cause of Christ. It's the Holy Spirit who connects us to the love of the Father[7] and convicts us of sin.[8] He is the truth-teller who helps us understand and trust in God's Word.[9]

When the Apostle Paul explains that Christians are "*being transformed*" by "*the Lord, who is the Spirit,*" (2 Corinthians 3:18), the verb "being transformed" is passive. In other words, transformation is done *to* us, not *by* us, and is only possible with the help of the Holy Spirit. The Spirit enables every one of us to live Christlike, fruitful lives and make the changes of heart, mind and lifestyle that will allow us to become more and more like Jesus. This is the normal Christian life.

God's work and our work

Fortunately, as we've seen, God does the heavy lifting in our process of transformation. He initiates and empowers us to become more like Jesus, and it's all by grace - it's his gift of love, freely given to us. We don't deserve it, we can't earn it, and without it, we can't bring about any lasting change in our lives to make ourselves more holy or more fruitful.

However, relationships are two-way. On the one hand, the life-transforming power of a relationship with God relies entirely on him; on the other hand, it relies entirely on our willingness to cooperate fully with his work in us. We have the immense privilege of sharing in the very nature of God himself, so that we can live as he calls us to by trusting in his promises in the Bible and accessing the resources he's made available to us. Our responsibility as disciples involves practice, hard work and effort over time. We must learn to freshly encounter God, surrender to his will and intentionally follow Jesus into the world. We need to *participate* in order to benefit from God's work in our lives.

Theologians have tried to describe this dynamic. It is not *synergism* (us working alongside God as if we have our own agency and power apart from God), and it's not *monergism* (God doing all the work, while we do nothing). A better word, coined by John Barclay[10], is *'energism'*, meaning God works within us by transforming our capacity to do everything. This enables us to engage with him in a joint transformation venture in discipleship, where our efforts and actions require God's grace and the 'energising' Holy Spirit.

In fact, God's grace and love not only transform but compel us towards love and good works. Grace is not like an external restriction or law that tells us the rules and regulations - rather it transforms us from within. The Apostle Paul tells his apprentice, Titus, that grace moves us to action - *'It teaches us to say "No" to ungodliness and worldly passions, and to live self-controlled, upright and godly lives in this present age,'* (Titus 2:12). Grace is active. Wine lovers tell me that tasting a fine vintage wine makes it ever so hard to return to the cheap bottle of plonk. As we taste the goodness of God, it reveals the emptiness of sin and our idols, and permanently ruins us for anything less. We can say 'no' to sins we once found attractive because our desires and appetites have been rewired from within.

Recently, I spoke with a friend who would have described herself a few years ago as a very average, run-of-the-mill sort of Christian. She was faithful and loving to her husband and children, she and her husband gave around ten per cent of their earnings to the local church, and she worked in a charity that helped disaffected youth find their way into employment. On the outside, she looked like a thriving, growing Christian, yet inwardly she was experiencing dryness and boredom in her faith. She had plateaued spiritually and felt that life was passing her by. She spent countless hours and wasted evenings endless scrolling on her iPad, lost in a world of fantasy and escape. No one knew this was what she did with her time, and she didn't even see it as a problem. She wasn't looking at anything technically sinful, but she was avoiding God and numbing the pain of her boredom and dryness with mindless entertainment.

One evening, however, she sensed the Holy Spirit leading her to confess her dryness and apathy to a trusted friend. As the two of them talked, she experienced a wave of sadness and conviction over her lack of care and concern for her own spiritual life, and began to realise that God had made her for so much more. She repented deeply and asked God, through many tears, to forgive her and help her change.

With her friend's help, she set some boundaries and expectations for herself. She limited her screen time and asked her friend to hold her accountable for spending time daily with God. She then made a simple declaration to God: "*I want to say yes the next time you ask me to do something.*" She didn't know whether she would manage to keep to this, given her recent track record, but she wanted to start living differently.

Over the next month, she felt God prompting her to phone a few friends, share her sorrow over her sin and ask them to pray for her. She also began to notice sinful attitudes in her thought life and immediately rejected them. She was suddenly participating in God's desire to change her from the inside out.

Even her husband noticed the change in her and started to make adjustments in his own devotional life.

Next, she sensed the Holy Spirit prompting her to start chatting with her neighbours. On one of her days off, she popped over for a cup of tea with an elderly man who seemed lonely. She shared a little of what God was doing in her life, and though he wasn't a believer, he said he'd like to start reading the Bible with her. One thing led to another and eventually, to her great joy and his, he became a Christian. This lady is now regularly prayer-walking her neighbourhood, asking God to help her find people who are open to hearing about Jesus.

For her, there is no going back to the old life of sleepy Christianity. As she ejected unhealthy thought patterns and habits, and embraced a simple attitude of obeying Jesus, she began to experience change on the inside. She stopped doing certain things and started doing others, and relied on Christian friends to help and support her. The outcome has been not only an inner change of heart and mind, but a new outward commitment to reaching out to others with the love of God and the message of Jesus. She is beginning to live this radical vision of discipleship for herself and her family, and she believes others can, too.

Defining Discipleship

What exactly is discipleship? It isn't just believing in God or claiming to be a Christian without there being any discernible impact on our character or lifestyle. Discipleship means following Jesus, like his first disciples in the gospels. The gospel of Matthew records Jesus' first instructions to them: *"'Come, follow me," Jesus said, "and I will send you out to fish for people.'"* (Matthew 4:19) "Following" also features in his last command to Peter before the Ascension, when he twice told him '*Follow me!*' (John 21:19, 22)

This following was not just a physical journey from village to village, but involved repentance, faith, theology, lifestyle, ethics, mission and spirituality, in sum, a total transformation to increasingly become like their Rabbi in every aspect of life.

The following wasn't just about obeying a set of rules or core teaching; it was concerned with imitating Jesus' way of doing life. This is why Jesus described himself as '*the way*'.[11] Jesus was the only way to access the kingdom of God and the only one to model their lives upon.

And the following wasn't about being part of an entourage, getting caught up in the commotion, admiring the miracles from a distance or consuming the teaching but not embodying them. Admirers are slightly removed and personally detached from the cost and commitment of wholeheartedly following Jesus who was the pattern for life and godliness.

Therefore, a ***disciple*** is a follower of Jesus, who is being changed by Jesus and is actively involved in the mission of Jesus. Disciples follow *and* copy Jesus. They have entered an apprenticeship with Jesus to become like him. They are not required to be spiritual, religious or respectable before they start this journey, rather anyone and everyone is invited to be captivated by Jesus and imitate him.

And ***discipleship*** is the word that describes the work of becoming like Christ and embracing his mission. It involves a continual surrender of every part of our lives to God's perfect design for us and a willingness to humbly admit we are spiritually poor.

That's why the word '***formation***' is currently used interchangeably with discipleship. We are being formed into Christ's likeness and joining his work in the world. We are taking on his character and increasingly living life as he would want us to.

Disciple-making happens when we actively help others to follow Jesus, be changed by Jesus and engage in the mission of Jesus. This is at the heart of the great commission - '*to go and make disciples*' (Matthew 28:18-20). When we create an atmosphere in the church that encourages everyone, all the time, in every way, to be a disciple-maker, I'd call that a ***disciple-making culture***.

Throughout this book, I will also refer to '*discipleship moments*'. These are particular moments when the Holy Spirit calls our attention to something specific that he wants to address or change in our lives. In one sense, all of life is a discipleship moment, as God's sanctification is an ongoing process, not limited to our '*spiritual*' moments; rather, he is always working. In a *discipleship*

moment, however, we have a 'eureka' experience in which we recognise that
God is getting our attention and inviting us to cooperate with him in making
a specific change in our thinking, attitudes or behaviour - another step forward
in our journey towards becoming like Jesus.

---

1. 1 Corinthians 6:9-11

2. Galatians 2:20

3. 1 John 4:7; 5:4–5

4. Colossians 1:28

5. John Stott, Preach on Colossians 1, 17th June
   2001, https://www.printandaudio.org.uk/app/search/resources/series/
   130/resource/1109/title/christian-maturity

6. John 14:16-18, 25-26, Acts 1:8

7. Romans 5:5

8. John 16:8

9. John 15:26

10. John Barclay, Paul and the Gift, (Eerdmans, 2017) p.442

11. John 14:6

"Your desire for more of God than you have right now, your longing for love, your need for deeper levels of spiritual transformation than you have experienced so far is the truest thing about you. You might think that your woundedness or your sinfulness is the truest thing about you or that your giftedness or your personality type or your job title or your identity as husband or wife, mother or father, somehow defines you. But, in reality, it is your desire for God and your capacity to reach for more of God than you have right now that is the deepest essence of who you are."

Ruth Haley Barton
(Sacred Rhythms: Arranging Our Lives for
Spiritual Transformation)

THREE

MY DISCIPLESHIP JOURNEY

As we will see in the coming chapters, understanding and paying attention to our lives, past and present, is crucial to the formation of our heart and character. Our upbringing, culture, environment and experiences all deeply shape who we are, and there are particular key moments in all of our lives that have had a disproportionate effect on us, for good or ill. It takes time to piece together our past and understand how it impacts our present life and affects the way we live as disciples of Jesus. When it comes to discipleship, our individual stories really matter.

Unpacking your story, however, can seem a daunting exercise, and it's sometimes helpful to hear someone else's story in order to better understand your own. Paul the Apostle spoke honestly about his life as a persecutor of Christians before he met Jesus.[1] He was also open about his weaknesses and failings,[2] describing himself as the foremost of sinners.[3] He talked about his past and his struggles in order to demonstrate God's grace in his life.

So at the start of this chapter, I want to narrate parts of my own discipleship journey, and of course, this feels fraught with challenges! I wouldn't want my openness to be interpreted as trying to win anyone's sympathy, or claiming that my experience is the best way to grow as a Christian. All I know is that understanding ourselves and piecing together our life story and God's activity in it, prepares us to respond better to the Holy Spirit's promptings in the future. I share some of my story in the hope of helping us do that.

Story-based discipleship

Imagine you're sitting with me in a discipleship group with seven others. The leader has just shared his story of God's work in his life. Beforehand, he had instructed the rest of us to come to the group prepared to give an account of our own lives thus far. I had roughly five minutes' worth of reasonably shallow thoughts about my history ready to share, but to my horror, he took an hour to explain his story, and clearly expected us to do the same.

Let me tell you, he was brutally honest. He was more open than anyone I'd ever heard about his failures, difficulties and weaknesses. He talked about the sort of things I tried to push deep down and hide from the world. He connected the pain and wounding in his life to the healing he found in Christ. He named the lies he'd believed about God and the gospel and how he'd learnt to replace them with truth from the Bible. And he talked about his past and present struggles with sin. I sat there open-mouthed, unable quite to comprehend this sort of vulnerability.

As he wrapped up, I glanced around the group and saw the terror on everyone's faces as it dawned on us that it would be our turn next. We squirmed in our seats and tried to laugh it off nervously, but it was exactly what I needed. It was what we all needed. Over the next few sessions, as I listened to my friends tell their stories, I tried to process my own. I slowly understood that I was far more messed up than I realised, which had massively impacted my growth into maturity.

My dad left home when I was two, and my sister and I spent several years being babysat by an elderly neighbour while my mum worked nights as an Intensive Care Unit senior nurse. As a vulnerable young mother, she was taken in by the Mormons, and I remember visiting missionaries who would come over to the house to entertain us and check up on her.

She remarried six years later, and sadly my new stepdad was incredibly insecure and had been deeply damaged by his own father. He refused to let my mum return to the Mormons, and our home life changed overnight. His insecurity meant that he saw it as his job to crush me into submission. He wanted to impose himself on our family, but failed to be the dad every eight-year-old desperately yearns for. I dreaded him coming home from work and finding something wrong with me or the house. He'd shout and unleash his anger on me, leaving me in pieces, and would moan to my mum about my behaviour when she returned from work. She would try to defend me, but he would then turn on her, which made me feel even worse.

This combination of strict rules and hostility meant I often knelt in front of him, begging for forgiveness for any wrongdoing, but forgiveness was never offered in return. As a result, I lived with the constant fear that I might cause my mum's second marriage to fail.

My mum worked hard to compensate for his lack of love, but I increasingly retreated from others in order to protect myself. I became expert at wearing a mask and never dropping my guard. I escaped into an inner world where I felt in control and gave nothing away, armouring up my heart and vowing many times never to let anyone hurt me again. I feared any vulnerability, yet was desperate to be loved and accepted.

I enjoyed being a leader, but because of my reluctance to expose myself to the risk of rejection, I preferred to be vice-captain in sports teams, and vice-president in clubs. In this way, I could indulge my sense of being a leader, but without the risk. I realised I was good at working out what people wanted from me and doing my best to give it to them. What I didn't realise is that when you pretend to be someone else for too long, you lose who you really are. Every relationship was saturated by my need to be loved, yet my fear of rejection placed me at a distance from everyone who I was supposedly close to.

After leaving school at eighteen, I went abroad for four months and returned to find my stepfather jaundiced and ill. Later, he was diagnosed with pancreatic cancer and he slowly died at home. I felt very little for him and, if anything, was keen for his dark shadow to be removed from our family. Even though I had made some inner vows to lock down my emotions in my early teens to avoid being hurt, inside I was furious at the way he had treated me. And behind much of this anger was a deep longing to be fathered.

During my teenage years, I had found refuge in the family of a school friend. Their home life was full of laughter and fun, and I enjoyed spending time with my best friend's dad. I saw my birth father every other weekend, but he was focused on his new family, his work and sport, so he felt distant and detached.

I regularly asked to stay at my friend's house at weekends, which provided an oasis of relief from my own home. Little did I know that this was a Christian family who were praying for me to know Jesus personally. They invited me to go to a Christian sports camp with their children, and it was here that I first heard about God's unconditional love for me. I realised that my sin separated me from him, and that Jesus Christ's death on my behalf offered me a way back to God. I didn't fully understand it all, but I knew it was true, so I responded with an inner '*yes*' to God.

Actually, the honest version is that in the first year of camp, I put my hand up to become a Christian because a girl I fancied all week put *her* hand up. But during my second year of hearing about Jesus, I knew he was real, and that his sacrifice was for me. As I prayed my first prayer, I felt God's love and peace, not just in a lukewarm, fuzzy way, but like a defibrillator sending jolts of acceptance deep into my bones.

Zombie Faith

It wasn't long, however, before the pain I carried kicked in, along with all my coping mechanisms, and I soon began to see God as another stepfather who demanded perfection and the keeping of rules. Yes, there would be moments of grace, spiritual highs where I'd gulp down God's mercy and make promises of devotion that would turn out to be short-lived. Most of the time, I simply felt that I was failing to satisfy my heavenly Father, just as I'd failed to satisfy my earthly one.

I learnt how to act as a good Christian young man, but inwardly, my heart wasn't in it. I felt dead on the inside, desperate for acceptance, locked down in shame and fear, with no one to guide me out of my inner prison. I was totally unaware of how my history had impacted my life and felt powerless to change. I felt shame at my sin, but was completely ignorant of why I did what I did. Within a few years I was, in practice if not in belief, agnostic. I had a zombie faith, in which I felt too guilty to relate to God, but too convinced of his reality to give up entirely.

I left for university excited about a fresh start for friendships and faith, but there was no escape from my inner confusion. I ended up living with some guys who hated anything to do with the church and who bullied me about my floundering faith. Like many others who've suffered abuse, I was repeating the cycle of hurt in a different place with different people. At some point, I was asked to lead the Christian Union and secretly had to give up my non-Christian girlfriend to accept the offer; I had fooled the Christians at university just as I had fooled everyone else. You won't be surprised to hear I decided to become vice-president (I was still too fearful to actually lead anything), and though I was zealous for people to hear about God, I felt lost and alone.

God, however, was still at work behind the scenes. A new church had started in the town only a year before I started university there, which appealed to students and was full of the most radically-minded Christians I had ever met. Their faith in Jesus impacted every aspect of their lives. They cared for the poorest in the town with love and dedication, and I loved to be near them when they worshipped God. They prayed, expecting God to listen, and they read their Bibles, confident that God would speak. Their Sunday meetings were terrific; I listened to the sermons, eager to learn rather than watching the clock. At the end of each service they would pray for each other, expecting the Holy Spirit to bring transformation and healing, but this felt too intense and personal for me – so after a time I left, and didn't return until about a year later, when someone invited me back out of the blue.

And after I'd been going there again for a few months, my world was jolted into a completely different orbit. One Sunday, some people spoke from the front, calling out individuals they felt God wanted to specifically encourage with particular scriptures. I had never encountered this practice before, but as soon as they began, I knew they would pick me.

I wondered if I could make a quick exit as my pulse began to race. I was terrified that this was the moment I would be exposed as a fake and my closet full of skeletons would come to light, when I'd worked so hard to present a healthy, normal life to anyone watching. But God knew what I needed, and lo and behold, I was picked out and asked to stand. The lady who'd picked me out spoke gently, and said that God knew me and had plans for my life. All these years later, I don't remember what else she said or the scriptures she quoted...but I distinctly remember what it *felt* like: I felt known. I felt God calling my name, despite the mess and pain of my life. I felt that God *wanted* me.

At the end of the meeting, I dragged myself to the front to receive prayer. I had never been prayed for by someone in person before. I was nervous and defensive. I tried to purify my mind by thinking of angels and heaven, but fortunately, someone realised I was looking apprehensive. They asked me to unfold my hands and hold them in front of me, as if I was about to receive a gift. As I relaxed externally, I said internally to God, "*Whatever you want to give me, I trust that it is good*".

They prayed for me to know God's love and be filled with the Holy Spirit. In that moment I suddenly experienced something like liquid peace filling my mind and then my body. I encountered a glimpse of the goodness of God that felt similar to when I'd first become a Christian, but this was different. Maybe I was thirstier than before. I left utterly changed, and I don't say that lightly. It was the most liberating day of my life. God knew me and loved me! I went home and suddenly wanted to read my Bible. I couldn't wait to worship and talk with God. All the things I knew I *ought* to do were suddenly things I *wanted* to do. I found a new responsiveness in me to obey God. I felt that everything I'd hoped of Christianity was *true*.

Removing my masks

And this was the story that I found myself telling, just a few months later, to the seven people in that small group, knowing that God had provided a safe place where I could unpack my pain and receive healing from him. It wasn't all sorted in that one evening - it was a process that took quite a long time. My fears were still present, but deep down, I was desperate to take off the masks, be known by others, and step into God's purposes for my life. There were many people to forgive and many things to be forgiven for.

Slowly, I gained insights into all the barriers I had put up against God. I started to unpick years of bad choices and habits. I noticed my lack of attachment to other people and tried to grow closer to friends. I also began to yearn for others to enjoy what I was experiencing. I realised that my presenting issues were governed by my deeper pain and coping mechanisms, the false self that I'd developed in all the years I spent pretending, avoiding and living on the surface. It was time to go deeper.[4]

The more I discarded pretence, the more I discovered my true identity in Christ. I wasn't just the sum of other people's thoughts about me, and I wasn't a powerless victim of my past. I was a son of God, made righteous by Jesus, whose brother I now was. I started feeling liberated, but fear still kept rearing its ugly head. Because of the rejection I'd experienced as a child, I desperately wanted people to like me, and I feared their opinions more than anything. I realised that to a large extent, my life was controlled not by me but by my fears. That was why I had allowed my housemates to mistreat me for years. My fear meant I was unwilling to try and stop them from walking all over me.

One afternoon, my friends from the discipleship group came over to the house for a cup of tea, where they endured thirty minutes of abuse from my housemates and were stunned that this was my reality. In our group meeting later that day, they questioned me about it. After listening to me Jeff, the group leader, encouraged me to confront my housemates and demand that they change their behaviour and attitude towards me. This felt like an impossible ask, yet I felt God wanted me to do it. I was slowly learning that joy is always on the other side of obedience, so I returned to the house.

When I got home, my housemates were watching television in the lounge, and I strode purposefully to the TV, switched it off, and declared, *"Guys, I've got something really important to tell you"*. Such was their lack of respect for me that one of them simply got up, reached behind me and turned the television back on. I couldn't believe it. Suddenly I saw their utter disregard for me. I immediately pushed the 'off' button with such force that I nearly knocked the television from its stand. I then raised my voice, pointed my finger at them accusingly and said with as much authority as possible, *"You will never speak to me or my friends like that ever again. Do you understand?"*

Tears were in my eyes, and my finger shook like a leaf, but I had finally done it. I had stood up to them. I said, *"You've been totally out of order, and I will never let you treat me like this again."* And then I left and went to my room. It was a momentous moment for me, having never stood up to people before. Over the next few weeks, if I'm honest, I'm not sure that any of them changed – but I knew that *I* had changed entirely. It was a first step of obedience to God. I had begun to fear God more than my housemates, and wanted more than anything to do what *He* told me to do.

Remember Lot's wife: Losing my life to save it

In this season, I was coming to terms with the call to be a disciple. Jesus says a remarkable thing in Luke 17:32-33, *'Remember Lot's wife! Whoever tries to keep their life will lose it, and whoever loses their life will preserve it.'*

The story of Lot's wife is found in Genesis 18-19. As the destruction of Sodom commenced, God instructed Lot's family to leave and not to look back and watch. However, Lot's wife couldn't resist the temptation. The Hebrew word translated *'looked back'* in the story from Genesis 19:26 means *'to look favourably upon'*. Lot's wife wasn't just looking back with interest to see what was going down; she was looking back with longing and regret, struggling to let go of her old life. Everything she knew and trusted lay within those city walls.

Her peace and comfort were there, her history, her friends, her whole life. All were being left behind, and God had instructed her to lose them in order to save herself. Sadly she couldn't. She didn't want to let go. She couldn't deal with the loss and doubted the God who wanted the best for her. As a result, she was turned into a pillar of salt and her calcified remains left standing like a monument to remind us not to make the same mistake.

In a similar (though somewhat less dramatic) way, God was calling me to lose my life in order to preserve it. Everything I had built to help me cope in life was built on faulty foundations. The '*good life*' I was leading was shallow and fake. I needed to surrender it to God. And I found that it was far more than a one-off decision, as things that I thought I'd left behind suddenly reappeared in my life. For example, in my teenage years, I'd been obsessed with my image. It was not just about my appearance, but about how I presented my life to others. I'd been so keen to impress others and receive their affirmation that I had perfected the art of giving people what I thought they wanted from me. It was an unconscious habit that affected every personal interaction.

As I tried to break free, I found it almost impossible not to return to pretending to be someone I wasn't. The coping mechanisms of pretence were deeply ingrained. My double-mindedness felt inescapable and the fear of rejection was intense. Every good intention was riddled with my need to be loved and even in my more honest and vulnerable moments, I was aware of how good my honesty looked to others. I couldn't win. This wasn't something that would go away with one heartfelt prayer. It would require a lifelong fight.

Every day became a fresh opportunity to change a lifetime habit, looking to God for my identity and acceptance instead of to others. I would store Bible verses in my pocket to meditate on when things got difficult. I would journal about my fear and ask God to help me focus on loving others rather than desperately wanting them to love me. I would regularly confess my sinful motivations to friends and ask for their help. I'd brace myself before meeting up with certain people I wanted to impress, and lean into God's approval instead. And when things got too much and I wanted to give up, I drew on the encouragement to '*Remember Lot's wife*'. Unknowingly, in these early years of discipleship, I stumbled on some of the most important hallmarks of Christians who experience transformation. *Surrender, Encounter and Obedience.*

Surrender, Encounter and Obedience

These three hallmarks of discipleship come in no particular order, but they help us define what a healthy disciple looks like. We probably spend our lives circling in and out of them, and they can all happen at the same time or one by one. Every disciple-making church will emphasise these three characteristics, though they might call them by slightly different names, and every Christian who is moving towards maturity will have embraced them.

We try to talk about them constantly at Mosaic. We preach on the themes of surrender, encounter and obedience, and we hope they will be embodied in leaders and encouraged and prized by everyone in the church. We have heard story after story of people who have gone through this journey, and it can become part of your discipleship journey too.

Please don't misunderstand – these three hallmarks are not a way of becoming a Christian or earning God's favour or becoming better people by our own efforts, but are a *response* to God's gracious invitation. Of course, we are saved by grace through faith alone. The effort required to walk in surrender, encounter and obedience is empowered by the Holy Spirit, and possible only through our union with Christ. However, embracing these three things is essential to a fuller, richer, deeper life in Christ—the life of a disciple-maker.

Of course, these three hallmarks only describe an *internal* posture that leads to change. Other external factors will also contribute. Major life transitions or crises often produce an impetus to change, as does the realisation that something is broken or not working well in our lives. Sometimes, it's the people around us who inspire us to change, or a mentor who doggedly believes in us and encourages our growth. Yet surrender, encounter and obedience remain at the essential heart of maturing in the way God invites us to. And over the next three chapters, we'll look at each in turn.

Questions

1. Are there any parts of my story that you can relate to? Take some time to write these down and ask God to show you how they impact your life.

2. Who are the people that inspire you most to follow Jesus - what are some of the characteristics of their life and walk with God?

3. Imagine Jesus asking you to '*Remember Lot's wife*' - what things do you struggle to let go of in your life? Why is it difficult to surrender those things to Jesus?

---

1. Acts 22:1-21; Acts 26:1-23; Galatians 1:13-20; Philippians 3:4-6

2. 2 Corinthians 11:30; 2 Corinthians 12:1-10

3. 1 Timothy 1:15

4. Peter Scazzero talks about the iceberg of self-understanding and how you need to go deeper to fully understand yourself - in Peter Scazzero 'Emotionally Healthy Spirituality: It's Impossible to Be Spiritually Mature, While Remaining Emotionally Immature' (Zondervan, 2017)

"According to Jesus, discipleship is not about self-actualization or self-preservation; it is about self-denial. You will know yourself the most when you are carrying your cross. All of our self-actualized visions of discipleship and our own little kingdoms need to crumble and be crucified if the kingdom of God is going to reign in our lives. True self-knowledge comes not through being true to yourself but through denying yourself."

J.T. English
(Deep Discipleship)

FOUR

HALLMARKS OF A DISCIPLE - SURRENDER

During the intense season of being discipled for the first time, I started questioning many of my life's choices. I felt I had wasted so much time. I had built everything on such poor foundations. I was also coming to the end of myself. It's hard to describe it, but the realisation of how messed up I was inside broke me. I felt powerless and fragile. It was embarrassing how far I had drifted from what was authentically me. And I had spent years pretending that I was okay.

I'd often made excuses or promised that things would be different in the future. *"Those things weren't really that bad". "Plenty of other people are far more messed up than me". "I just had a bad day."* Yet now the game was up. I couldn't deny it any longer. I had finally hit the end of myself. My sense of brokenness humbled me, but it felt both terrible and wonderful as I knew God was doing the breaking.

I've learnt that when a horse gets broken in, it's a process by which the horse is taught to submit to its true master (which is ultimately for its good). That's the brokenness that flowed into me. It was this strong sense of connecting with the reality of my sinfulness and immediately leaning into God's grace-filled leadership over my life. It was overwhelming yet comforting.

Surrender is where we realise the state of our sin and the immensity of God's holiness and love. Our eyes are opened to the realisation that we are like dust without him. We are entirely unqualified. His way, not ours, is the best. His mission, not ours, is the true purpose of our lives. We know very little and are nothing without him. Because of this, surrender has to be at the heart of discipleship.

Jesus models surrender

Think of Jesus. He holds nothing back to redeem humankind. Think of his entrance and exit in ministry. He surrenders to the waters of baptism and immediately finds the joy of his Father's voice, crying out his delight in his Son. He then submits his will to the leading of the Holy Spirit, who sends him into the desert. The devil then questions his identity and offers him the world. Jesus resists these temptations, leaning obediently into the Word of God and emerging from the wilderness resolved to do his Father's will. Then later, as the cross looms, Jesus again finds himself alone in Gethsemane, gladly surrendering his life to God's will. '*Not my will, but yours be done.*' (Luke 22:42)

Surrender is simply following in the footsteps of Jesus. As pastor and author E. Stanley Jones said, '*Self-surrender is at the very heart of God and is at the very heart of all his attitudes and actions. When he asks us to surrender ourselves he's asking us to fulfil the deepest thing in himself and the deepest thing in us.*'[1] In other words, our surrender echoes the surrender found in Jesus.

Broken before the Lord

Many of us have a negative cycle that gets repeated again and again in our lives. We feel pain, so we escape to a destructive or addictive habit. We feel relief, but the relief fades away, and we're left to experience shame, guilt and all the consequences of our behaviour.

Surrender starts when we admit to ourselves that this doesn't work. We try to stop going round the same old cycle of pain, escape and guilt, and find we're unable to. We come face to face with our failure, rebellion and powerlessness, fall to our knees in conviction and repentance and turn to God, and as we connect with our weakness, we allow pride and self-sufficiency to give way to humility. We begin to submit more fully to God and to his purpose for our lives.

We see the seeds of surrender in the story of the prodigal son as he licks his lips at the thought of eating the pigs' food. Suddenly he comes to his senses and realises it's his own bad choices that have led him away from his home and family.[2] We see the first fruits of surrender in Zacchaeus' life as he repents and gives away his ill-gotten gains in response to his encounter with Jesus.[3] And we see a deeply loving surrender in the worship of the woman who broke an alabaster jar of precious perfume to anoint Jesus before his death.[4]

We too can connect with our selfishness, emptiness, foolishness and faithlessness, with the mess we've made of relationships and life choices, and surrender in repentance. And like the woman with the perfume, we too can surrender things that have been precious to us, because we've found a greater prize in the person of Jesus. This is the beautiful yet challenging path to being broken before the Lord.

Whatever our past looks like, today can be the day to start over. King David understood this, even after committing adultery and murder. *'My sacrifice, O God, is a broken spirit; a broken and contrite heart you, God, will not despise.'* (Psalm 51:17) This sort of brokenness doesn't mean wallowing in our mistakes and guilt, or being full of self-loathing or self-pity.

In Dane Ortland's book 'Surprised by Jesus' he asks, *'Are Christians to be broken? Well, it depends what we mean. If by 'broken' we mean downcast, long-faced, perpetually discouraged, handwringing, abject, ever grieving over sins - no. If by 'broken' we mean contrite, low before the Lord, poignantly aware of personal weakness, self-divesting, able to laugh at ourselves, having sober judgement, being sensitive to the depths of sin within us - yes.*[5] And it isn't a one-off event. Brokenness is living in ongoing awareness of both our sinful condition and God's grace. It's a continual posture of humility and contriteness on the one hand, and dependence on God's grace and goodness on the other.

Author Nancy Leigh DeMoss helpfully explains that brokenness involves shattering our wills, stripping self-reliance and softening the soil of our hearts. She pictures the vertical and horizontal dimensions of brokenness as a house with the roof off (brokenness towards God) and walls down (brokenness towards others).[6]

The prophet Isaiah experiences this sort of brokenness and surrender when he encounters the weight of God's glory and holiness. *"'Woe to me!' I cried. "I am ruined! For I am a man of unclean lips, and I live among a people of unclean lips, and my eyes have seen the King, the Lord Almighty."*(Isaiah 6:5) Isaiah is a broken man, and it will open the door of his heart to God's love and purposes for his life.

The first funeral I conducted as a pastor was for a wonderful young man who tragically died in a car crash. His wife was devastated by her loss and grief; she shook with deep sobs of anguish and loss every time I saw her. Her parents held onto her at the funeral to keep her from running out. As I stood before the congregation, we projected a photo of her husband onto the screen, and she simply wailed as she glanced up to the picture. It was a deep groan of pure grief and sorrow, rippling out through the crowd like a tsunami wave. It said, *"My life is over; I'm as good as dead without him"*. This is the cry, the *'woe'* Isaiah groans as he sees his own frailty and sinfulness in the light of the glory and holiness of God, and it leaves him broken. He feels as good as dead, yet God's grace awaits him. Maturity is about growing more aware of our unworthiness, not less, as this opens us up to the only One who can make us worthy.

Yielding our rights

Spiritual formation needs to happen in the places where we are most unlike Jesus. All of us are fragmented, our hearts divided. Parts of our lives are surrendered to Jesus, while other parts are not, and we will remain rebellious and fragmented as far as we refuse to allow him to be Lord. Like an unbroken horse, we like to run free and be in control, rather than admit that we're often imprisoned by our own sinfulness and inadequacy and not really in control at all. It makes me wonder whether we have resolved the question, "*Who is in charge?*" Do we think of Jesus as an advisor whose words we can take or leave, or as the King whose rule we live under and whose words we submit to?

Our experiences of life and the world we live in often combine to tell us never to give away the keys of our autonomy to others, and we may have been badly hurt in the past when we've done so. Surrender to Jesus, however, is placing our lives in the purest and safest hands in the universe. Jesus will never deceive us, abuse us, exploit us or abandon us. He is absolutely faithful and absolutely loving. And as we submit to his authority and his word, we experience the paradox of true freedom that increases as we increasingly submit our lives to him.[7] Surrendering our autonomy to him starts a chain reaction, unlocking other parts of our lives that are yet to be under his servant-hearted leadership.

Another term for surrender could be '*yieldedness*'. In England we have '*give way*' signs to instruct drivers to submit or defer to the oncoming driver. In America, these are called 'Yield' signs. If you decide to ignore these instructions, there will be a collision or confrontation with another driver. Yieldedness to God is where we submit, defer our rights, and give way to him.

Love and Yieldedness

Yieldedness connects us to both God's unfathomable love for us and his distress at our sinful choices. When Simon the Pharisee had the gall to question Jesus' acceptance of a sinful woman washing his feet with her tears, Jesus said, "'*Therefore, I tell you, her many sins have been forgiven—as her great love has shown. But whoever has been forgiven little loves little.*'" (Luke 7:47) Jesus didn't deny her sin but overwhelmed it with his forgiveness.

Those who have plumbed the depths of failure, repentance and brokenness dig a well deep enough for the love of God to come rushing in. Those who feel they don't need much of God's grace fail to receive it and fail, in turn, to give it away. Jesus said, '*It is not the healthy who need a doctor, but the sick. I have not come to call the righteous, but sinners.'* (Mark 2:17) A surrendered person holds both hands high above their heads and says from the heart like the tax collector *'Lord have mercy on me, a sinner'* (Luke 18:13).

Sadly, I've met people who, like Simon the Pharisee, refuse to surrender themselves fully to God's mercy. They want to hold onto their life, their priorities and identity, and indeed, it's all too easy to base our sense of identity in our problems and difficulties as well as in our achievements, possessions and status.

Sally is a huge advocate of transformation and healing, but doesn't ever seem to find that healing for herself. She talks about the rejection she's experienced and can get very emotional in small groups, leaving the room in tears when something has upset her. She talks about how the church has failed to care for her and for other hurting people, and yet, like Simon, she is unaware of how self-righteous and judgmental her own behaviour is, and of her need to repent and surrender to God's mercy. Her sense of identity is so bound up in her emotional neediness that the very area she needs to open up to God's mercy is the very thing she doesn't want to surrender.

Sally seems to regard God as a kind of therapist whose job is to meet her emotional needs and assuage her pain. If only she were willing to understand that he is her Father who loves her deeply. If only she would surrender her wounded and rebellious heart to him, she would begin to find her freedom, discover her true identity as a beloved daughter of the King of kings, and to love him more deeply, like the woman who washed his feet with her tears.

Yieldedness is a pridebuster

I won't be able to surrender to God unless I first shed my wrongly placed self-confidence. The Stoic philosopher Epictetus said, *"It is impossible for a man to learn what he thinks he already knows."* Surrender requires a humble acknowledgement of need and a lifelong commitment to handing control back to God, like the Apostle Paul had a healthy downward trajectory in his thinking. He describes himself as *'the least of the apostles'* when writing to the Corinthians.[8] A few years later, he says, *'I'm the least of all the Lord's people.'*[9] And then lastly, when writing to Timothy, *'I'm the least of all sinners'.*[10]

One of America's greatest theologians, Jonathan Edwards, described what happens when we dethrone our agendas and rights, *'A truly Christian love, either to God or men, is a humble brokenhearted love. The desires of the saints, however earnest, are humble desires: their hope is a humble hope; and their joy, even when it is unspeakable, and full of glory, is a humble, brokenhearted joy, and leaves the Christian more poor in spirit, and more like a little child, and more disposed to a universal lowliness of behavior.'*[11] Yieldedness is a pride-buster. It kills the Pharisee in us that wants to earn God's grace through living a life of outward obedience without inner repentance and surrender. It stops us from feeling qualified to be used by God and re-orientates us to the fact that only Jesus qualifies us before God.

Wonderfully, in this broken ground of submission, God finds fertile soil for his plans and purposes. God's grace tastes sweeter to those who connect with their utter need for salvation.

Surrender involves an exchange

I've learnt that surrender and yieldedness are precious gifts that God gives us to offer back to him. Even though surrender may be costly and painful, we always get something better in return. Surrender is like compound interest for the soul. We need to remind ourselves of this at every step, as the consumer culture around us tells us to take control, acquire, and possess. It can powerfully influence us into putting ourselves at the centre and making choices *my* way, for *my*self, on *my* terms.

Surrender is an emptying which leads to a filling. Jesus declared, *'What good is it for someone to gain the whole world, yet forfeit their soul.'* (Mark 8:36) God's world is full of wonderful and beautiful riches for us to experience and enjoy, and we are fortunate if we have freedom and means to do so. Yet this is not the goal of a surrendered disciple of Jesus. Instead, our little lives find their fulfilment within God's love and purposes, and this is the true antidote to consumerism. As we resolve to surrender our whole selves to God, we will find new life and new desires are birthed. We truly relinquish our lives in order to find them. We are truly buried with Christ in order to be raised with him.[12] You could say, *"A disciple is one who actually gets on the cross. Not one who simply believes in the cross or is grateful for Jesus's cross. A disciple is one who follows Jesus so closely that they take up their cross. Their life has taken on the same shape as Jesus. To be a disciple is to be cruciform."*[13] Of course, our cross isn't one of atonement, of attempting to pay for our sins. Jesus has done that for us, once for all, and we have no need to punish ourselves! Rather, our cross is one of self-denial, costly surrender and dying to our old life, the life without God in charge. We die to playing it safe and we die to our attempts to control God's role in our lives.

I once discipled a woman who was the daughter of missionaries. She had grown up in and around the church and felt colossal pressure to please her parents and lead a model Christian life. However, she rebelled at school and found herself in a peer group that regularly slept around and took drugs. She perfected the art of enjoying a hedonistic Friday night followed by a holy Sunday morning.

She knew how to fake Christian maturity, even to the point of leading worship and Bible studies whilst taking cocaine the night before. She somehow justified this double life in her own mind, though she knew deep down that it wasn't ok. She prayed many times, promising that she would change and live a clean life, but she always returned after a short time to her addiction to drink, drugs and sex, and her double life continued for many years. By the time she came into our discipleship group, she had all but given up expecting things to be any different.

She liked her wayward life, and the thought of holiness bored her. She talked about her chameleon-like existence, and we discussed different options. But the most pressing issue was that she didn't really show any remorse or sense of repentance. She had no concept of how God saw her life and sin. She knew her parents would be horrified if they found out, but that wasn't enough to reform her. We asked her to spend some time reading Isaiah chapter 6 and asking God to reveal himself to her.

The following week she had transformed into a different person. She had spent each morning dutifully reading about Isaiah's experience of God, but initially, nothing had happened. Yet, out of the blue, God had spoken to her almost audibly. His words came like thunder, "*The enemy keeps inviting you to dinner and you need to stop accepting his invitation. It stops and it stops now.*" Suddenly, God had answered her prayers and revealed himself and his hatred of her promiscuity and drug taking, and it broke her. Seeing the beauty of his holiness caused her to bow down before him and freshly surrender her divided heart. With this yieldedness came a hatred of the life she had previously enjoyed. It suddenly tasted foul in her mouth and mind. She understood that compromise and double-mindedness were empty and dissatisfying compared to the riches of intimacy with God.

Confidence in the goodness of God

Surrender happens when we are confident in the goodness of God's character and secure in his love for us. In his excellent commentary on John's Gospel, Frederick Dale Bruner notes that the three times God's voice is heard, he is affirming his love for his Son, Jesus. [14] At the same time, each declaration from heaven follows a profound moment of humility in which Jesus surrenders his rights and his agenda and obediently submits to the Father's salvation plan. First, he submits to baptism as an example to us, though he had no sin to repent of or be forgiven for.[15] Second, he is firm in his decision to go to the cross, which is followed by the Father's affirmation of him at the Transfiguration.[16] And third, he says as he enters Jerusalem, that the time has come for him to become the grain of wheat that dies in order to produce many seeds.[17] Each time, we *hear* the Father publicly approve of his Son, and each time we *see* deep, confident surrender. Wonderfully, this means that when I believe that I am God's beloved, it enables me to confidently lay down my agenda and priorities.

Repentance

Surrender will also naturally lead to repentance. Jesus began his ministry with these words *"The kingdom of God has come near. Repent and believe the good news!"* (Mark 1:15) and his last recorded words, speaking to the churches in the book of Revelation, are *"Those whom I love I rebuke and discipline. So be earnest and repent."* (Revelation 3:19)

I've heard someone compare their battle with sin to a jungle monkey trap. Hunters place delicious monkey treats in a container with a hole just big enough for the monkey to reach its open hand into. However, the hole is too small for the monkey's closed fist to be pulled out holding the treat. The monkey refuses to open its hand and give up the treat and so remains trapped by its desire!

My battle against sin feels similar. So often, I refuse to let it go, trapped by my own sinful desire. I need to open my hands and let it go, humbly admitting my sin and changing my mindset and behaviour, rather than trying to carry on as if nothing is wrong. This is where repentance kicks in - we need to make a deliberate choice to let go of sinful thoughts and actions and turn towards Christ.

Repentance is a wholehearted change – but not just an intellectual one. Look at the call to repentance found in the book of Joel. *"Now, therefore," says the Lord, "Turn to Me with all your heart, with fasting, with weeping, and with mourning." So rend your heart, and not your garments; return to the Lord your God, for He is gracious and merciful, slow to anger, and of great kindness; and He relents from doing harm."* (Joel 2:12-13) Notice that God does not call them to tear their garments (external behaviours) but to tear their hearts (godly sorrow for sin with a desire and intention to change).[18] If we change our *outward* behaviour without *inward* change that comes from the Spirit's conviction, we are simply coping and pretending. Jesus was clear, change the heart, and our life will also fall in line.

Repentance, then, is a change of mind and heart that leads to a changed life. It's a God-given, deep, lasting, "coming to your senses" sort of experience. Our internal attitude or mindset turns through 180 degrees with the result that our outward words and actions also turn through 180 degrees.

Think of King Josiah, who burnt the priests' bones to destroy the idols in his nation.[19] He took no prisoners but eliminated all remnants of the pagan priests' existence. Are we equally ruthless in ridding ourselves of the things we look to and depend on in place of God? Some may be good things in themselves that we have grown to place an unhealthy dependence on, and we perhaps need to fast from them for a season to break the dependence and "return to the Lord".

Repentance may be difficult and involve tears, but it leads to joy because it calls us back into God's best for our lives. It's admitting *"I've gone to the wrong places and people to satisfy me and meet my needs"*. It's feeling gutted but not being consumed by guilt.

Writing 1600 years ago, John Chrysostom encouraged us, *'Be ashamed when you sin, don't be ashamed when you repent. Sin is the wound, repentance is the medicine. Sin is followed by shame; repentance is followed by boldness. Satan has overturned this order and given boldness to sin and shame to repentance.*[20] Repentance is actively trusting that God's way is truly what we're made for and turning towards it, freshly receiving God's forgiveness, healing, restoration and a renewed vision of the love of Christ. It's both sweet and painful.

This part of repentance can also involve making amends, apologising, putting things right, and wisely reaching out in love to those impacted by our sin, as Zacchaeus did. During a simple meal with Jesus, he encountered unlimited love and mercy which, in turn, empowered him to confess, repent and pay back those he had robbed.[21]

Growing at the speed of repentance

Over the years, I've found that mature Christians are quick to repent when they find themselves drifting from God. Early in our discipleship journey, we can find ourselves lingering in sin, saying to ourselves, "Well, I've sinned once, so I might as well carry on sinning for a while!" or "I shouldn't have done that, but God will forgive me, so it doesn't really matter... I'll carry on doing it for a while."

It's like a child who had broken into the cookie jar and, having eaten one cookie, carries on and scoffs the lot. Author Jen Wilkin comments, "*Sanctification rarely looks like an immediate ceasing of a particular sin. It more often looks like an increase in the distance between repeated sins, and a decrease in the distance between committing them and confessing them. God is so patient with his children.*"[22]

If we're growing as disciples, we'll find that we start to love the things that he loves. We become more aware of our identity in Christ, we become increasingly uncomfortable about continuing to sin, because it's not who we are any more. We used to be slaves to sin, so that sin used to be our default. But now we're slaves to righteousness, our default is to do what is right, and sin feels increasingly uncomfortable.[23]

Repentance as a road to freedom

Repentance and breaking with the past is also a powerful tool for finding freedom from sins committed not *by* us but *against* us. Often we have taken on board lies and unhelpful behaviours in response to other peoples actions towards us. Repentance offers a way to escape their ongoing impact.

My friend Mark had always struggled with self-confidence. He had been part of a large church staff team that was led by a controlling leader. The feedback he received for his work was often harsh and brutal, his willingness to work long, unsociable hours was ignored, and other people got praise for some of his best work. When Mark talked about himself, he couldn't find anything good to say. He had embraced the lies spoken over him and felt worthless.

As we unpacked his story and the many ways he had been mistreated, he realised his complicity in believing what his leaders had spoken over him. He had let their lies find a home in his heart. Quietly, we spent time praying together and I encouraged him to repent of these thoughts he'd believed about himself. He spoke out the lies and renounced them. He claimed the biblical truth about himself and his competency and announced them over his life. And the change was immediate. You could see the cloud of despondency lift from him as the

Holy Spirit revealed his true delight in him. Mark is now a different man in the workplace. His confidence is rooted in his identity in Christ, not the criticism of an abusive church leader.

No surrender: No maturity

Let me be blunt. I've never met a mature disciple who is full of pride and self-sufficiency. I've never met a mature disciple who hasn't experienced both the depths of sorrow over sin and the heights of wonder and gratitude at God's grace. And I've never met anyone who became a mature disciple overnight! It takes a long-term lifestyle of surrender to Jesus for our rebellious and selfish nature to be transformed into Christlikeness. And if we only surrender a little, we will only grow a little.

I remember when God first asked me to surrender to him in my bedroom at my student house. In the quiet, I felt prompted to give my whole life over to God to do as he pleased. As I prayed, I wanted to make it real and tangible and consecrate myself to God. Given that I was sitting among all my worldly possessions, I asked God what he wanted me to keep and what he wanted me to give away.

It was an unusual time of clarity, repentance and liberty. I opened my wardrobe and looked at the clothes - many of the designer names and brands that I used to create my image needed to go. I then looked at my extensive CD collection and asked God, "*Should I let them go or keep them*"? Gently I felt God say, "*Give them away*". I immediately knew why. Just as I'd used clothes to give me a certain image, I'd tried to find identity by listening to certain types of music, and it dragged me away from my true identity in Christ. It wasn't that my clothes or CDs were wrong. You'll be glad to hear that I still own and wear clothes; instead, I realised that Jesus had something better for me, freedom from wanting to impress others.

As my eyes crossed the room, "*My stereo?*" I whispered. It was a really good one and I dreaded having to give it away. "*Yes, keep it*", I felt the Father say, and silently, I cheered inside. And so it went on, covering everything I had in this life.

I finished that time feeling light and free. It has helped to break my attachment to material things and develop my willingness to continually surrender my life, belongings and dreams to God.

Daily surrender

While surrender may start with a life-changing moment, it doesn't have to. What's important is the call to follow Christ every day. It's a process of daily surrender that lasts our whole life. It isn't limited to our belongings but extends into every nook and cranny of our life. It is a wilful choice to relinquish control, rights, or property. It means, *"God, I have stuff (ideas, plans, desires, relationships, possessions, and objectives), and I give it over to You for You to take and do with all of it what You will."* Every decision, every goal, and every moment becomes an opportunity to put God first. Though they may fail often, disciples who grow in this habit have positioned themselves for growth and Christlikeness.

This is why surrender is a prerequisite for disciple-making—true yieldedness defeats self-sufficiency and breaks down our resistance to the Holy Spirit. We surrender because we recognise that we bring nothing to the table and are utterly dependent on God. Only he can transform us. Only his grace can save us. Only God. In turn, this breaks the power of idolatry, where we look to other things to do what only God can do. It opens the doorway to a deeper experience of forgiveness, meaning and purpose. All told, this means that one of our main tasks in discipleship is to convince people (including ourselves) that surrender is worth it and to help people keep yielding themselves daily to our wonderful God.

Questions

1. Can you identify any areas of your life where you ring-fence and avoid surrendering to God? Why do you do that? What are you worried about losing?

2. What does surrender look like to you? What do you think you'll receive if you lower your defences and let Jesus be the Lord of your life? Write out what you think you'll receive in exchange for your surrender.

3. In what ways do you trust God the Father and his purposes for your life? Can you identify areas in which you struggle to trust him? Bring your worries and doubts to God in prayer.

---

1. N. T. Wright, 'Simply Jesus' (London: SPCK, 2011), p. 7.

2. Luke 15:11-31

3. Luke 19:1-10

4. Matthew 26:6-13

5. Dane Ortland 'Surprised by Jesus' (Crossway, 2021) p.94

6. Nancy Leigh DeMoss 'Brokeness, Surrender and Holiness'(Moody Publishers, 2008) pp.44-45

7. Ephesians 6:6

8. 1 Corinthians 15:9

9. Ephesians 3:8

10. 1 Timothy 1:15

11. Jonathan Edwards, 'Religious Affections', (Yale, 1959), p. 339

12. Romans 6:4

13. Packiam, Glenn. 'The Resilient Pastor', (Baker Publishing Group). Kindle Edition. p.149

14. Frederick Dale Bruner 'The Gospel of John' (William B Eerdmans Publishing Co, 2011)

15. Matthew 3:13-17

16. Matthew 17:1-13

17. John 12:24

18. 2 Corinthians 7:10

19. 2 Kings 23:20

20. translation Gus George Christo:The Fathers of the Church vol. 96: St John Chrysostom: On Repentance and Almsgiving - Homily 8

21. Luke 19:1-10

22. Jen Wilkin tweet, 3.28pm, April 13th, 2021 https://twitter.com/jenniferwilkin/status/1381977579494727686

23. Romans 6:17-19

"God inhabits our bodies, delighting in every inch of us. Every eccentricity and peculiarity is received. Every longing and self-destructive habit is known. God knows us through and through and still wants to make his home inside of us. The fact that the Holy Spirit wants to abide in us is one way we know how infinitely precious and beloved we are. We are God's own prized possessions. Prized possessions are something you take care of."

Adele Ahlberg Calhoun
(Spiritual Disciplines Handbook:
Practices That Transform Us)

FIVE

HALLMARKS OF A DISCIPLE - ENCOUNTER

After graduating, I moved into a rented house with a couple of other guys from church, including my mentor, Jeff. He showed me how to do the basics of the Christian life by living it himself. He spent time with God daily, was an avid reader, and pushed me to study scripture. He even started a men's running club that doubled as a memory verse tutorial. He wanted to get us physically fit while imprinting scripture into our memory. We would spend some time together after the runs and talk openly and honestly about our relationship with God.

Jeff helped me through what I'd describe as *'life on life'* discipleship. Many pastors use a model of formation focused on *"come and meet with me"* whereas the Bible often presents disciple-making as *"come and do life with me"*. The unspoken expectation was *"follow me as I follow Christ"*.[1] We learn far more from what we see than what we hear. My discipler showed me how he followed Jesus and inspired me to do the same.

Living with my discipler meant discipleship wasn't reserved for special moments but happened *in* the moment. I had a bad habit of stretching the truth and lying to present myself in a better light, and he lovingly confronted me each time I did it. He saw how I lived and gently nudged me into making better choices. He noticed when I failed to come through on a promise and showed me the impact of careless words. He'd confront my inappropriate attitudes toward people and help me think biblically about my priorities and habits.

I was quickly shown that disciple-making involved investment in others. I loved talking with other young men about what I was learning and how they could start their own disciple-making journeys. We learnt how to confront each other and give honest reflections to one another. In our immaturity, sometimes these were a little brutal, or we'd project our own issues onto others, but the climate of radical honesty and acceptance meant we formed life-long friendships. We started to shed ungodly habits and addictions that had plagued our lives for years.

My discipler also wanted us to share Jesus with our friends and neighbours. We were happy to try anything – enduring a seemingly fruitless afternoon knocking on doors trying to find people who wanted to chat about God. I can't say that we were very successful, but we certainly pushed through some of our fears. Eventually, our missional attempts morphed into an outreach evening at a local pub, which consisted of long chats into the night in which we talked about God and the gospel and ended up praying for some people.

In this season, I started to ask God about my future and remembered that when I'd first walked into a church building aged fourteen, I'd intuitively sensed that one day I'd help lead churches. At that time, however, I was far too scared to stand in front of people and actually lead. I didn't want that sort of responsibility or face my fear of people not following my leadership. As I began to mature, I felt it was time to embrace this calling and stop making excuses. So one evening, I opened up to a trusted friend and as we talked, a vision for a disciple-making church came spilling out of my mouth. I had never verbalised this dream before and I was left a little stunned and wondering if God was in it. The following day I was introduced to a lady known for her ability to hear from God. She told me, *"God wants you to know that he has called you to lead,"* and then repeated everything I'd expressed the night before, almost word for word. It was a profound, life-changing moment. God was confirming publicly things that I'd been thinking privately and reluctantly. This encounter with God filled me with new confidence and motivation to devote my life to him, to discipleship and to growing churches embracing a discipleship culture that transforms lives locally and globally.

The importance of Encounter

For the disciple, surrender, which we looked at in the previous chapter, doesn't stand alone. It's coupled with encounter, by which I mean the ongoing experience of the Holy Spirit and the Word of God transforming us and drawing us deeper into a relationship with Jesus the Son and God the Father. Encounter is the natural partner to surrender. As we empty ourselves, God fills us with his Spirit, and we're awakened to his work in us and in the world.

When the Apostle Paul explains his mission to the church in Rome, he underlines both his own role in sharing the gospel with people *and* the Holy Spirit's role in their sanctification. *'He gave me the priestly duty of proclaiming the gospel of God, so that the Gentiles might become an offering acceptable to God, sanctified by the Holy Spirit.'* (Romans 15:16) The word of God brings us the truth we need, and the Spirit of God instigates and empowers our transformation.

In his book 'Movements That Change the World', Steve Addison asserted, *'History is made by men and women of faith who have met with the living God.'* [2] Simply put, we are so incapable of change by ourselves that only by encountering the Trinity can wholesale root and branch transformation occur. This has been God's method since the creation of humanity. Every major biblical character and leader can point to a life-changing, ongoing encounter with God that marked their lives forever. It may have happened in a moment or over a lifetime of deepening intimacy, but all change starts and continues only through God's intervention and ongoing presence.

The Power of Encountering God

Isaiah's role as a prophet starts with a powerful encounter with God. He tells us, *'In the year that King Uzziah died, I saw the Lord seated on a throne, high and exalted,'* (Isaiah 6:1). The words are simple but the experience was life-changing. Isaiah was completely overwhelmed by the sight of God's glory and authority. He sees him seated on a throne, a picture of calm, unthreatened authority. Parents of young children know that there isn't often much time for sitting down - only when everything is sorted and done and under control can they finally rest. God, however, is eternally seated on his throne because he is supremely in charge and nothing disturbs his authority and rule.

Isaiah catches only a glimpse of God's awesome greatness: *'...and the train of his robe filled the temple,'* (Isaiah 6:1). Just as it's impossible to look directly into the centre of a bright light, Isaiah can only see what is round the edges of God's presence - the bottom of his robe - and even that is enough to fill the Temple.

'Above him were seraphs, each with six wings: With two wings they covered their faces, with two they covered their feet, and with two they were flying.' (Isaiah 6:2) Seraphs are not like the chubby baby angels we sometimes see on Christmas cards, but are flaming beings whose name means *'burning one'*. Perhaps the white-hot glory of God sets them alight, and they cannot help but burn. Yet even they dare not look directly at God but cover their eyes; and they do not feel worthy of their privileged position, so they cover their feet. And as they speak, the temple shakes. (Isaiah 6:4) *'At the sound of their voices the doorposts and thresholds shook and the temple was filled with smoke.'*

It would take a lot to shake the stone thresholds and massive doorposts of the Temple - the sound must have been deafening. And what are they saying? *'"Holy, holy, holy is the LORD Almighty; the whole earth is full of his glory,"'* (Isaiah 6:3).

Holy is the word we use when other words fail to describe someone totally different, pure, set apart, perfect, and unique. And God is not just holy, but *'holy, holy, holy.'* Three times holy describes a level of utter, unique holiness that can never be equalled. And while the outside edge of God's glory is filling the

Temple, the seraphs reveal that the full extent of his glory is more than enough to fill the entire planet.

Isaiah knew God before this encounter, but after it, he *knew* God.

This '*knowing*' isn't just intellectual knowledge (though it is that as well). When the Apostle Paul reminds the Corinthians they have received the Spirit in order to understand what God had freely given them in Christ, the Greek word he uses for 'understand' is '*oida*', which refers to experiential knowing, in contrast to intellectual understanding.[3] Paul is not checking if the Corinthians know about God's grace by taking an exam or test, but asking them to remember that the Spirit wants us to encounter the full measure, the overflowing, never-ending, unconditional love pouring from God's heart, given freely through his grace. Like Isaiah, we are to *know and experience* God, not merely learn information about him.

The Father heart of God

Though no one has seen God, we come face to face with him in Christ. The writer of Hebrews tells us, '*The Son is the radiance of God's glory and the exact representation of his being,*' (Hebrews 1:3) and Jesus himself explained, '*"Anyone who has seen me has seen the Father"*' (John 14:9). Wonderfully, we are invited to encounter the Father, through Jesus, by his Spirit.

The author Michael Reeves argues that the most foundational thing about God is not some abstract quality but the fact that he is Father. He claims, '*Since God is, before all things, a Father, and not primarily Creator or Ruler, all his ways are beautifully fatherly. It is not that this God 'does' being Father as his day job, only to kick back in the evenings as plain old 'God'. It is not that he has a nice blob of fatherly icing on top. He is Father. All the way down. Thus all he does he does as Father. That is who he is. He creates as Father and he rules as Father; and that means the way he rules over creation is most unlike the way any other God would rule over creation.*'[4]

This means we can trust and delight in his rule over the universe and over us. It means God the Father, by nature, is like a fountain, ever flowing with love for his children. Fatherly love is not something God has, or a job he does; it's who he is. God *is* love.[5]

God isn't a moody or unpredictable Father, nor is he distant or removed. He is absolutely consistent in his unchanging love. God the Father has loved the Son eternally[6], and in the Son we too are loved. In fact, in Jesus the Son, God the Father has so lavished his love on us that he has adopted us and made us his sons and daughters. To know that we are loved by the Father in the same way that he loves Jesus changes us profoundly and breaks the power of thinking like a spiritual orphan.[7]

Orphan thinking

Orphan thinking is the mindset that leads us to the false belief that God, though possibly benevolent, is essentially distant or uncaring. The resurgence of the glorious truths of the Father heart of God and our adoption in Christ can speak powerfully to generations who have experienced the pain and difficulty of having absent, missing, uncaring or abusive fathers.

We have seen breakthrough after breakthrough as people have come to understand and experience the reality of the Father's love for them, and their new identity as his sons and daughters. God's heart is that no one should be left a spiritual orphan. Whether we have had a good earthly father or not, we all need the love of our Father God, and he longs to welcome us home and lavish his love on us.

Jewish children call their mum '*Imma*' and dad '*Abba*'. Similarly, the Holy Spirit connects us to Father God so profoundly and intimately that our spirits cry out '*Abba, Father*'.[8] There is nothing formal, prepared, controlling or manipulative in this cry. It's direct from our hearts, just as children call out to their parents.

As God's adopted children, we come to know that we are the apple of his eye[9], and his delight and joy. Henri Nouwen states this truth simply - '*Spiritual identity means we are not what we do or what people say about us. And we are not what we have. We are the beloved daughters and sons of God.*'[10]

Several years ago, my friend Lisa was woken early in the morning by an actual audible voice calling her name three times from downstairs. She thought it must be God, so she went downstairs and spent time with him, and he started speaking to her about his passion for vulnerable children and adoption. She wrote in her journal a few Bible verses about God's heart for orphans and started praying for vulnerable children. But at the time, she was pregnant with her third child and so didn't think that adopting a child was something she would be in a position to do herself.

Within three years, however, Lisa did in fact adopt a young boy, and at the time he joined her family, she remembered how God had spoken to her and wondered if the date of that encounter had been significant. It wasn't her adopted son's birthday, but she checked through his records and found it was the day the court had ruled that he would be removed from the care of his birth parents: it was the day her son had become an orphan.

God saw that young child in the moment of his greatest need, and God sees us right now, no matter how desperate or alone we feel. It might feel as if no one is aware of our plight. But God's eyes are on us. He sees us and loves us, just as he was there with Lisa's son before she knew him. He doesn't leave any of us as orphans. Instead, his desire is to father us in a way no earthly father ever could.

Learning to live as sons and daughters

The Father, Son and Spirit have worked together to bring us into sonship. Look how Paul carefully describes each of their roles in your salvation. *'But when God, our kind and loving Saviour God, stepped in, he saved us from all that. It was all his doing; we had nothing to do with it. He gave us a good bath, and we came out of it, new people, washed inside and out by the Holy Spirit. Our Saviour Jesus poured out new life so generously. God's gift has restored our relationship with him and given us back our lives. And there's more life to come—an eternity of life! You can count on this.'* (Titus 3:4–7 - The Message)

Apparently, when three defenders go up against someone in basketball, it's called being triple-teamed. I like to think the Trinity has triple-teamed undeserving people (like me and you) to pull us into God's family. God delights to welcome us home. He conspires to enfold us in his arms.

These days, we use gender-neutral and inclusive language, yet the Apostle Paul boldly calls all of us 'sons'.[11] In Roman times, it was normally only male children who inherited status and wealth, but Paul subversively declares that everyone, male and female, has the same rights of inheritance. Paul uses the idea of sonship as a metaphor for the glorious inheritance and identity bestowed by God on every believer, male and female.

I've found that understanding and experiencing our status as 'sons' becomes the key to unlocking rejection, fear, and disappointment. We all have 'father wounds,' as none of us had perfect fathers. However good and loving they may have been, even the best fathers fail to model God's perfect fathering of us in its entirety. This means we all need, deep down, to encounter God's perfect love and reframe what we think a father is like.

Brennan Manning challenges our wrong thinking about God: '...if we continue to picture God as a small-minded bookkeeper, a niggling customs officer rifling through our moral suitcase, as a policeman with a club who is going to bat us over the head every time we stumble and fall, or as a whimsical, capricious, and cantankerous thief who delights in raining on our parade and stealing our joy, we flatly deny what John writes in his first letter (4:16)–"God is love." In human beings, love is a quality, a high-prized virtue; in God, love is his identity.'[12] Once we know and feel the delight of being God's son or daughter, it acts as a soothing balm for the 'lack' in our hearts. The particular father-shaped hole we have in our hearts begins to fill up, expand, and heal when we encounter the Spirit.[13] We begin to realise that we're daughters and sons, not slaves.

This sort of fathering gives us confidence in our true identity. It stops the tailspin into feeling worthless, unlovable, forgotten and pushed aside. It means we don't have to defend ourselves when criticism or rejection comes, or push back in arrogance and pride, which are other ways of dealing with a sense of worthlessness. Instead, as we increasingly learn to live in our true identity as adopted children, it gives us the security to withstand the storms of self-rejection.

We *are* God's children, and we are slowly *embracing* our status as God's children and learning to live in the good of it. We need to let the knowledge that we are God's sons and daughters invade our thoughts, actions and feelings, and one way of doing this is to regularly celebrate and be thankful for all that it means to us. We were loved before anyone hurt or wounded us.[14] God chose and accepted us before we came into existence. We were wanted before anyone rejected us.[15] Our names are carved into the hands of God.[16] Every hair on our heads is counted and there is no place to escape God's loving, watchful Spirit.[17] Encountering the Father is the high calling and privilege of every Christian.

Learning to feel loved by God

Some of us may be like Steve, who had been a Christian for several years but struggled to feel God's love. His father had been emotionally distant and demanding, and nothing Steve did was good enough for him. All this meant that Steve lived with a constant sense of worthlessness and self-doubt. He had struggled with anxiety and depression all his life and even contemplated suicide at times, wondering if his life mattered to God. He asked me, "*Does God really love and value me and if so, why is he so distant?*"

I explained how our emotional responses are often under-developed when we've grown up in an environment where they were never modelled or demonstrated healthily. This lack of emotional expression can mean that we don't feel things very deeply or that our emotions are limited to anger or hatred that sometimes spill out of us in an uncontrolled way. It's no surprise we feel distant and unloved by God when we grew up with a lack of love and closeness and consequently suppressed our own emotions for a long time. Gently, I encouraged Steve to learn to recognise and express his emotions while simultaneously asking God to reveal his love for him.

Over time, Steve began to recognise different emotions and give room for them to be expressed. He started to write down his feelings and express them to God. We spent time thinking about his father and how important it was to forgive him for mistreating him and failing to express his love for him. He also began to use his devotional times to invite the Holy Spirit to fill him with peace and love. Gradually, he sensed a growing intimacy with God. He loves Jesus' story of the two sons,[18] and particularly identifies with the older brother who never realised how much his father loved and valued him.

Steve looks visibly different now when he enters a room. Instead of shuffling in, trying not to be noticed, his head is lifted and he makes contact with his friends as his confidence in his value and worth as a son of God grows. He still struggles at times to sense God's love for him, but there has been a gradual breakthrough into freedom from the habitual sense of worthlessness and depression that once defined him.

How to encounter the Holy Spirit?

So how does it work? How does our great and loving God touch our lives by his Spirit? Understanding the practicalities of how this happens is essential for helping us move from theory to practice. We recently spent a whole weekend at Mosaic giving permission for people to ask questions about encountering God. I was struck by both the hunger for an authentic experience of God and the nervousness some people felt around these issues.

Church members asked about how to avoid emotionalism and the worst excesses of hyped or pressurised meetings. They wanted to know how faith works when we ask for the Holy Spirit to fill us, particularly if we don't feel anything. One person asked, *"Do we fake it till we make it?"* Others asked, *"Do we simply wait endlessly to feel something?" "How does God work with our defences, emotional immaturity and fears?" "How do you process where you think you've been manipulated in meetings?"* These are such good questions. Let's start by considering the nature of God and his presence in our lives and then we'll find some answers.

God's Omnipresence

God is omnipresent; his presence is everywhere, at all times. David famously asked numerous questions about whether he could escape the presence of God. *'Where can I go from your Spirit? Where can I flee from your presence?' 'To the heavens? To the depths? The far side of the sea?* (Psalm 139:7) and finds that his attempts to flee from God are fruitless - there is nowhere where God's presence isn't. God is everywhere, all the time. And only God is omnipresent. All other beings are restricted to a given place at a given time. The devil, angels, and demons are all limited to a given time and space. Not God; there is no place or person too far for him to reach.

God's Indwelling Presence

God's presence inhabits our lives through the Holy Spirit. He lives in us. We could say that God unpacks his suitcase and makes his home in us.[19]

Jesus once gave a quick theology lesson to Israel's teacher, Nicodemus, in John 3. Jesus explains that no one can enter the Kingdom of God without being born of the Spirit. For Jewish people, being born was not as important as being born into the right family. They believed that God accepted people born into Abraham's family, and that was what really mattered.

But now Jesus is saying that God is starting a whole new family in which ordinary birth isn't enough. It won't qualify you any more. You must be born all over again, born from above and born of the Spirit and water. In other words, baptised in water and baptised in the Spirit.

As he explains this, Jesus is drawing on prophecy given by the Spirit centuries earlier to one of Israel's greatest teachers, Ezekiel - *'I will sprinkle clean water on you, and you will be clean; I will cleanse you from all your impurities and from all your idols. I will give you a new heart and put a new spirit in you; I will remove from you your heart of stone and give you a heart of flesh. And I will put my Spirit in you and move you to follow my decrees and be careful to keep my laws.'* (Ezekiel

36:25-27) Ezekiel prophesies that there will be a day where those born of the Spirit will receive a new heart, new cleansing, new spirit and new obedience. This day arrived when Jesus first sent the Holy Spirit to his church.

The Apostle Paul affirms that Christians are no longer controlled by the sinful nature when the Spirit of God lives in us.[20] Christ Himself dwells in our hearts through faith.[21] We are the temple and dwelling place of God.[22] No longer are Christians required to ask the priest to enter the temple and presence of God on our behalf. Remarkably, the Holy of Holies is now in us!

God's Manifest Presence (Immanence)

As well as being both omnipresent and indwelling, God's presence can also *manifest* itself. The God of everywhere likes to show up somewhere. This reminds us that God does not isolate himself from the world but rather is present and involved in people's lives.

All through the Bible, we find God enters his creation in a clear and specific way. Several times in Exodus, God reminds his redeemed people, trudging towards the promised land, that he has chosen to dwell among them.[23] There are also several occasions when people encounter God's manifest presence in the Old Testament: Abraham's three guests[24]; Jacob's wrestling opponent[25]; Moses' burning bush[26]; the commander of the armies of Joshua[27]; Manoah and his wife (the parents of Samson)[28]; the fourth man in the fire with three Jewish boys in the furnace[29].

Shift to the New Testament, and God's presence finds its greatest manifestation in Jesus. Seeing Jesus was like seeing the Father.[30] And when Jesus returns to the Father, he promises to send the Holy Spirit to be with his people and empower them for mission. This coming of the Spirit happened at Pentecost, and meant that the church, the people of God, was now the primary place where God's presence would be found, indwelling every believer, and at times manifested among them.

This all means that God is omnipresent, indwelling and sometimes reveals his manifest presence. There is a subtle difference. Theologian A.W. Tozer explains,

'The presence and the manifestation of the presence are not the same. There can be the one without the other. God is here when we are wholly unaware of it. He is manifest only when and as we are aware of His presence. On our part there must be surrender to the Spirit of God, for His work is to show us the Father and the Son. If we cooperate with Him in loving obedience, God will manifest Himself to us, and that manifestation will be the difference between a nominal Christian life and a life radiant with the light of His face.' [31]

Jesus promises to send the Holy Spirit to every believer.[32] In one sense, God's presence never leaves us, yet, sometimes, we are suddenly consciously aware of his presence with us - his manifest presence. This helps us understand why we can often pray for God's manifest presence but only sometimes *'feel'* he is with us. Every time we ask God to encounter us, we take a step of faith. We're trusting in Jesus' promises to send the Spirit.

Ongoing encounter by the Spirit

According to Paul, we can be filled with the Spirit regularly, like the wind filling the sails of a boat.[33] He tells us to *'walk in the Spirit'* and be *'led by the Spirit'*.[34] Notice he doesn't say, *'Follow the Spirit.'* He emphasises our lack of power and reliance on the Spirit's power and leading. He's not saying walking in the Spirit is like a cycling peloton where the Spirit is out in front making it easier for the chasing pack to pedal. (It's 30% easier to pedal when you're behind the lead cyclist.) This would give the impression that we have some power and ability of our own to follow and keep up, and that the Spirit just makes pedalling easier. But walking in the Spirit is much more like being a carriage behind a train engine. The Holy Spirit is the engine, and we're the carriages. On our own, we have no power. We cannot move or follow unless we hitch or couple ourselves to the engine. The engine or the Spirit pulls us along.

So, to walk with the Spirit is to couple yourself by faith to his power. And that enables you to love God and others as you love yourself. You may have built some momentum if you're not attached, but you'll eventually come to a standstill or go backwards. Being continually filled with the Spirit sanctifies and changes us into Christ's likeness.[35] We can do this as individuals and corporately as a church family.

Fresh encounters with the Holy Spirit create a renewed sense of spiritual health among believers, leading to personal and corporate renewal. This must go hand in hand with a passion for scripture and seeing the Bible as the foundational authority and guide for life.

Make room for encounter with God

Over the years, we've discovered this at Mosaic: God will encounter us if we create room for him. If we spend all our time entertaining ourselves, using up our energy and passion on other stuff, we won't be encountering him. He loves our hunger and desperation but exits a room filled with arrogance and self-sufficiency. This means turning our phones and screens off from time to time. It sometimes means drawing away from the things that steal your passion for God. By limiting them, you create space for the Holy Spirit to fill.

While I don't want to overemphasise feelings, I know that a tangible experience of the love of God heals hearts like nothing else. Encounter convinces people of the reality of God's love and acceptance and moves them forward in discipleship.

However, the Spirit doesn't force himself on us. We've found that if we're emotionally immature or find it hard to express emotions, it's unlikely (but not impossible) that we will be over-emotional when filled with the Spirit. However, as emotional freedom increases, as we trust God and understand his Word, we're more likely to 'feel' God's love for us.

It also means we have something to give away to others. It means our evangelism is not just focused on apologetics but also offers people something to experience. We've seen people far from God on our Alpha courses suddenly encounter his living presence, and it rocks their world. I remember a young man called George, who had regularly been invited to church by his housemate throughout his three years at university. He finally agreed to come but was still very reluctant and highly antagonistic towards Christians. He promised to punch anyone in the face if they told him Jesus loved him!

At church, he heard about Alpha and started coming to my house with half a dozen others to participate in the course. He was sharp, and people followed his lead. His arguments against Christianity were credible, and I'd often feel the frustration of him leading others against my carefully worked-out arguments for the life, death and resurrection of Jesus.

Finally, the Alpha day came, when we taught about the person and work of the Holy Spirit, and in the last session, we offered the chance for people to become Christians and prayed for people to encounter God's love. After around twenty minutes of praying, our team left the peaceful room of Alpha guests who were enjoying the presence of God.

George told us later that he had prayed his first prayer as we left the room. He said, "*God, if you're there, I want you to speak to me and show me if you're real. I don't want to believe it because Matt or others tell me I should. I want you to reveal yourself to me*". Suddenly God imprinted two numbers on George's mind, three and seventeen, which was beautiful as George was studying maths at university, and God chose to speak to him for the first time through the language of numbers.

As George sat there, wondering what three and seventeen had to do with anything, he opened his eyes and looked at the Bible we had given him. He'd already turned to Acts 2, the story of Pentecost, and suddenly saw the chapter and verse numbers, and quickly turned to Acts 17:3. In answer to his question about whether or not Jesus is real, Acts 17:3 says, '*...This Jesus I am proclaiming to you is the Messiah,*'. He encountered the living God through the Bible and subsequently gave his life to Christ.

Sabbath

Another way to encounter God is to regularly set aside time to joyfully re-member God wants to be with you. The practice of sabbath keeping - taking twenty four hours to reconnect with God and rest from work is making a comeback. Increasingly we're becoming aware that the relentless pace of life requires intentional time to decompress and detox. Many of us feel chronically exhausted and emotionally unhealthy. We can feel stuck in our spiritual journey but don't have the energy to do anything about it.

The word 'sabbath' means 'to stop and rest.' In Genesis, God worked for six days but then he rested on the seventh. In doing so, he built a pattern for us to follow. We all need time, once a week, to stop, rest and enjoy the presence of God. Resting on the sabbath isn't necessarily loafing on the sofa all day, scrolling through TikTok or your app of choice. Sabbath is about resisting the temptation to find rest in the wrong things and pursuing the peace and joy only God can provide. It's a 'holy' day meaning it's set apart for us to delight in life with Jesus and with others. Practising the sabbath creates space for us to encounter God.

Encounter with Jesus the Son

Not only does the Spirit reveal the Father to us, but he is sent out by the Father to reveal Jesus the Son to us. Jesus explained this in John 15:26. '*"When the Advocate comes, whom I will send to you from the Father—the Spirit of truth who goes out from the Father—he will testify about me."*' The Holy Spirit loves to reveal the person of Jesus again and again.

The impact of encountering Jesus left twelve young men so radically altered that when Peter and John were called before unbelieving and cynical religious leaders, they took note they had been with Jesus.[36] John Stott once lamented the church's lack of depth and maturity that stems from our failure to see and encounter Jesus. He said, '*We are pigmy Christians because we have a pigmy Christ. Our maturity, the level of our maturity, depends on the clarity of our vision of Jesus Christ.*'[37] It seems the greater the revelation we have of Jesus, the greater our maturity.

And we are closer to Jesus than we dare believe. Wonderfully, according to Dane Ortland, the Jesus we see in the gospels describes himself as '*Tender. Open. Welcoming. Accommodating. Understanding. Willing. If we are asked to say only one thing about who Jesus is, we would be honouring Jesus' own teaching if our answer is gentle and lowly*.[38] When we encounter Jesus, we come face to face with love, humility, joy, solidarity, sympathy, gentleness and unending grace. In fact, the further away from God, the more sinful and unworthy we are, the greater is the desire in the heart of Jesus to come near to us.

Beholding Jesus

When we *see* Jesus, transformation can happen. The great Puritan pastor Richard Sibbes wrote: *'The very beholding of Christ is a transforming sight. The Spirit that makes us new creatures, and stirs us up to behold this servant, it is a transforming beholding...A man cannot look upon the love of God and of Christ in the gospel, but it will change him to be like God and Christ. For how can we see Christ, and God in Christ, but we shall see how God hates sin, and this will transform us to hate it as God does, who hated it so that it could not be expiated but with the blood of Christ, the God-man. So, seeing the holiness of God in it, it will transform us to be holy. When we see the love of God in the gospel, and the love of Christ giving himself for us, this will transform us to love God.*[39] Encountering Jesus, Sibbes is saying, cannot fail to change us. We see his love, and we love. We see his holiness, and we long for holiness. We see his hatred for sin, and we hate sin. We see his surrender, and we surrender. We see his mission, and we embrace his mission.

Reverent Fear, Comfort and Joy

What does it feel like to meet with Jesus? Encounters with God's manifest presence often result in us feeling a mixture of reverent fear and comfort. Comfort comes as we realise the depth of God's love for us, but reverent fear comes as we are awakened to God being so much more, and ourselves so much less, than we thought.

We have been created for God's pleasure. We've been made to enjoy the deep, satisfying joy of communion with him. I love that Christianity isn't just about duty but about knowing God's smile. I long for those moments when we feel his tangible presence, he transforms and empowers us, and there's genuine acceptance and peace. Jesus is present in the sacraments; he is present in our prayers; he is present when two or more gather in his name. Our worship of Jesus reorientates our priorities and willingness to make sacrifices. Adoration drives discipline. Praise cultivates courage. Being captivated by Jesus increases our motivation and desire to live an obedient life.

For me, aged twenty-one, my first encounter with God was that deep dive into his peace and love as I stood slightly awkwardly at the front of a church meeting, trying to think of angels. Quite simply, it was a life-altering filling of God's Spirit. I was so thirsty for more of God but utterly unaware of the depth of my need for his presence and power. As several people came and prayed for me, I felt I had entered the Holy of Holies and found an outstretched hand offering what my soul needed most - God's presence and unconditional acceptance. That experience whetted my appetite for an ongoing encounter with God, through his son Jesus, by the Holy Spirit.

Disciple-makers are familiar with surrender and encounter. Each day is an opportunity to meet with the living God and be satisfied. This sort of life leads naturally to obedience, which is the subject of our next chapter.

Questions

1. How do you feel after reading this chapter? When would you say you last had an encounter with God? What happened? What did you feel? Did God say anything to you? What was its impact and fruit in your life?

2. How much do you want an encounter with God? Do you have any questions or hang-ups that would stop you from pursuing God in this way?

3. How can you grow in receiving the Holy Spirit in an ongoing way? How could you grow in your hunger for more?

1. 1 Corinthians 11:1

2. Steve Addison, 'Movements That Change the World: Five Keys to Spreading the Gospel' (Downers Grove, IL: InterVarsity Press, 2011), p.37.

3. 1 Corinthians 2:12

4. Michael Reeves. 'The Good God: Enjoying Father, Son and Spirit'. (Paternoster Press, 2012) p. 5

5. 1 John 4:8

6. John 17:24

7. Galatians 4:4-7

8. Romans 8:15

9. Psalm 17:8

10. Henri Nouwen, "Bread For The Journey", (Harper SanFrancisco 1996) p.210

11. Galatians 4:6-7

12. Brennan Manning, 'The furious longing of God' (David C Cook Publishing Company, 2009), p.77

13. Romans 5:5

14. Psalm 139

15. Ephesians 1:11

16. Isaiah 49:16

17. Matthew 10:30

18. Luke 15:11-32

19. John 14:23

20. Romans 8:9

21. Ephesians 3:17

22. 1 Corinthians 6:19-20

23. Exodus 29:45-46

24. Genesis 18

25. Genesis 32:22-32

26. Exodus 3

27. Joshua 5:14-15

28. Judges 13

29. Daniel 3

30. Hebrews 1:1-3

31. A W Tozer, 'The Pursuit of God' (Aneco Press, 2017) p.232

32. John 6:37-39

33. Ephesians 5:18

34. Galatians 5:16;18

35. 2 Corinthians 3:18

36. Acts 4:13

37. John Stott, Preach on Colossians 1, 17th June 2001 https://www.printandaudio.org.uk/app/search/resources/series/1 30/resource/1109/title/christian-maturity

38. Dane Ortland, 'Gentle and Lowly', (Crossway, 2020) p.21

39. Works of Richard Sibbes, vol 1, (The Banner of Truth Trust, 1979), p.14

"Joy, not grit, is the hallmark of holy obedience. We need to be light-hearted in what we do to avoid taking ourselves too seriously. It is a cheerful revolt against self and pride."

Richard Foster
(Freedom of Simplicity: Finding
Harmony in a Complex World)

Six

HALLMARKS OF A DISCIPLE - OBEDIENCE

Let the training commence

After university, I began an internship with Kings Arms Church in Bedford, UK and started my theological training. Shortly afterwards, I fell in love with my future wife, Philippa. I quickly discovered that marriage is a perfect setting for intense sanctification.

Most of our marriage was good, but our main problem was that we didn't know how to handle disagreement. For Philippa, any conflict growing up at home had resulted in violence and fear. For me, any dispute had resulted in rejection. It was a devastating cocktail. When we hit a point of tension, my insecurities would dominate while Philippa would shut down emotionally. I'd begin a conversation trying to find a resolution (while desperately seeking her acceptance and love), and she'd do the opposite of what I needed to make me feel safe. She'd back off and fall silent. There was no reassurance—just numbing silence. Asking, *"How are you doing?"*, would be met with thirty minutes of tumbleweed. She couldn't look me in the eye and was petrified I'd get angry and hurt her. It took all her energy to simply stay in the room, while every second of her silence reinforced my sense of rejection and heightened Philippa's fear. This was not the marriage I'd signed up for.

Together, we somehow managed to find a way through. Little by little, we began to talk about how conflict made us feel and tried to surrender our nearly uncontrollable coping mechanisms to God. Piece by piece, we worked through our issues, reminding each other that every conflict was a doorway to deeper engagement with the refining that God was doing in each of our hearts.

Starting in Leadership

Those first years of marriage were accompanied by my first experience of church leadership. The founding pastor of King's Arms moved away, and I was asked to step into his role just a couple of months after getting married. I was 26, leading a large, vibrant church and loving almost all of it, at least for the first couple of years.

After a while, I grew increasingly frustrated at the lack of growth and salvations. I turned to an emerging group of pastors from the US who were exploring new forms of church. Sadly, this quickly descended into a deconstruction of the church and the gospel. I sensed I was losing everything I held dear, including Jesus, in my well-intentioned search for fruitfulness.

Fortunately, Philippa and I were invited to spend time with friends who loved Jesus more than anyone we knew. Here we saw, up close and personal, a disciple-making culture that was healthy, growing and doable. It was astonishingly simple - their three values were to love Jesus, love others, and change the world, and this was reinforced, modelled and multiplied in every leader and ministry throughout the church. This church had seen thousands impacted by the gospel locally and had sent out over a hundred church planting teams in twenty years to some of the most dangerous parts of the world. We came home full of faith for transformational discipleship and a call to go church planting.

Four years earlier, when we'd agreed to lead King's Arms, we'd had to put any thoughts about starting a new church on hold. Even though we were desperate to go, we sensed that God wanted us to stay. It was a great lesson in blind obedience. At the time, it was confusing as to why we shouldn't just rush off to start a church, but looking back, God used this time to help us learn, mature and prepare as leaders. When we sensed it was time to move, we were both excited and relieved, but we didn't know where to go. We visited a few different cities in the UK, trying to figure out where God wanted us. Eventually, we drove to Leeds, explored the city centre and immediately sensed faith for this amazing city. Evangelical church-goers in the county of Yorkshire only numbered 1% of the population, so the need was huge, and we were excited about starting afresh.

Finding my identity

Our daughter was eighteen months old when we moved to Leeds to start Mosaic Church, and our son was born a month later. At first, we were on our own. No team, no friends, no money. Just a family of four trying to survive. Even though there were many long, depressing and lonely days, we knew God wanted us there. At times we longed for the comfort of familiar friends and a church where we felt known. We even had to take a photo collage down from the wall as our daughter would point at her friends' pictures and start crying. She was expressing how we all felt.

Philippa would often sob her way to various groups for mums and babies - they felt unfriendly and impenetrable, yet they were the primary ways she had for getting to know people.

I was struggling too. Having failed to find any work related to my skill set, I spent ten hours a day in a call centre. Without a church to lead, I spent my spare time with the family or prayer walking. It felt good to start a church entirely from scratch, yet I could sense a more profound work happening. About eighteen months in, I realised that God was making sure my identity was firmly in him, not in what I did or who I knew or what I had or how good my ministry was.

The realisation wasn't sudden – it was more akin to a dawning sense that God had orchestrated the whole situation and had removed all the usual supports in order to deal with my heart. This was important, because I wanted to take the credit for being a radical church planter, and base my sense of worth in that, but God had an alternative (and better) plan to make me humble and secure in him. My worth wasn't in my leadership of a prestigious church, nor in being a church planter (and seemingly a modest and relatively useless one so far!) It was in Jesus! It sounds obvious and straightforward, but it's an altogether different story when it moves from theory to reality. Even though I was very aware of my brokenness and pain, I had forgotten how easy it is to shift my primary allegiance away from God to myself.

By the end of our first year in Leeds, we had found just four friends who'd tentatively agreed to join our embryonic community. Every church planter I've met has done better than that, but we were happy. We met each week and began to disciple those whom God had sent us. Eventually, by the end of our second year, four had become twenty-four and we were gaining some momentum. Mosaic Church was finally getting started.

The Pressure of Parenting

As the church grew, we found God's crucible for transformation was our home life. If anyone thinks of themselves as spiritually mature, spending a prolonged amount of time with children is likely to bring about a serious reassessment! Children, whether they arrive naturally or through fostering or adoption, are a delight, a blessing and a privilege. And one of those blessings is that they are God's refining fire for their parents and carers. They expose whole areas of our characters that had remained neatly hidden away before.

Our own parenting style is usually informed by how we were parented. I struggled to shake off the strict, controlling, authoritarian approach I had grown up with. I found myself focusing on minor instead of major things. Rather than picking my battles, I made *everything* an issue, an opportunity to bring correction or discipline.

At moments of stress, my coping mechanism was to lock the situation down by exerting control over everything. It was my way of surviving. If I could be in control, then everything would be okay. My sense of well-being was firmly rooted in ensuring the children conformed to our standards of behaviour. However, children do not always obey, but often seem to enjoy rule-breaking and chaos and this pressed my buttons!

Fortunately, I was self-aware enough not to pressure them into submission through force or extreme punishment –but the lack of control made me feel exposed and uncomfortable. I would get angry and raise my voice when the kids failed to comply. Sometimes I'd walk off and want to punch a wall or stand in the corner of a room with my head in my hands, utterly frustrated. I found myself regularly apologising for losing my cool or being too strict with them.

In my struggle, I realised how good my parenting partnership was with Philippa. She was the opposite of me. She was happy to let the kids do their own thing. She was relaxed and chilled out, even inviting them to make a mess and explore their creativity. She also knew when it was time for me to tap out and tag team our parenting.

All this was an opportunity for God to reveal where my sense of peace and security was grounded. He showed me how deeply our ingrained behaviour patterns run and how much work is required to think and act differently. I shared my struggles with friends, who encouraged me to regularly take time out with God to process and review my fathering. I had no idea entering parenthood would reveal so much brokenness.

Resistance

The combination of marriage, parenting, and church planting in a new city was the perfect environment to learn increasing obedience to Jesus. Given the intensity of life and the vulnerability of pioneering in a new context, it felt that God was speeding up our formation. During this season, we would take turns every six weeks to have a short, twenty-four-hour retreat. We could rest, take a breath and commit ourselves afresh to submitting to God's loving leadership.

Even though we were keen and motivated to experience transformation, I could feel myself becoming resistant and stubborn. Even when I was outwardly cooperating and adhering to the rules, I sometimes burned inwardly with re-bellious desires. I wanted to do things *my* way, in *my* time, at *my* choosing.

We often want to negotiate our obedience and play by our own rules, but obedience has always been the hallmark of discipleship. Jesus commanded us to teach new disciples '*to obey his teaching*'.[1] According to Jesus, the mark of genuine followership with God was obedience, "*If you love me you will obey my commands*"[2].

When we cross the threshold of realising that our behaviour, attitudes, and desires must be aligned with Christlikeness, obedience is the only way to get there. Such is the potency of obedience that Christian writer Max Anders makes an astonishing claim, '*The shortest distance between us and the life we long for is total obedience to Christ.*'[3]

A hidden life

Last Christmas, Philippa and I borrowed a projector and watched one of the most beautiful films we've ever seen on the big screen. It was the Terrance Malick film, '*A Hidden Life.*'[4] It tells the story of a conscientious objector, who lived in Austria during the second world war. Initially, he was safe from conscription, but eventually, he was ordered to swear an oath to Hitler before joining the army. He refused and faced imprisonment and execution. Over time, priests, police officers, politicians and prison guards pleaded with him to capitulate. "*It's only words. God doesn't care about what you say; it's the heart that matters.*" "*Why do you think anything you do or say will impact the course of the war? No one will hear about you. You will vanish. No one will care.*"

Yet Jägerstätter stood his ground, refused to compromise and eventually, after a long imprisonment, was beheaded. Initially, his resistance seemed so futile. Nobody cared that he stuck to his principles, and his obedience seemed meaningless. His countrymen criticised him heavily for failing in his duty as a husband and father, the authorities refused to put his name on the local war memorial, and his wife was denied a pension. And yet when his remarkable bravery eventually came to light, his life continued to speak. The Trappist monk and peace activist Thomas Merton included a chapter about Jägerstätter and his incredible courage and endurance in his book 'Faith and Violence', and The Roman Catholic Church beatified him and declared him a martyr.

Philippa and I felt freshly inspired as we watched this beautiful film about one man's quiet obedience in the face of opposition. It struck us afresh that our secret acts of simple love may be hidden on earth but they are seen in heaven. When we ask, *"Does our mundane obedience make a difference?"* we can be assured that we are sowing into a life that matters to God.

The film takes its title from George Eliot, who wrote, *'The growing good of the world is partly dependent on unhistoric acts; and that things are not so ill with you and me as they might have been, is half owing to the number who lived faithfully a hidden life, and rest in unvisited tombs.* [5] All of us are called to live a hidden life of obedience. I doubt very much whether anyone will visit our gravestones, yet God highly prizes obedience. Every Christian is called to live an obedient life that is made up of minute, seemingly insignificant decisions that form us over time into mature disciples of Jesus. As we are faithful in the little things, God entrusts us with bigger responsibilities.

We like our sin

Sadly, we all fall short of this. As author Kevin DeYoung puts it '*We like our sins and dying to them is painful. Almost everything is easier than growing in godliness. So we try and fail, try and fail, and then give up.'* [6] It has been said many times that the difference between the Western church and many of the church planting movements we have seen around the world can be summarised by the word 'obedience'. Our Western teaching and training programmes emphasise *learning,* while church planting movements look for *obedience.*

Spiritual growth in the New Testament is measured not by what we've learned but by whether we've obeyed what we've learned.[7] The greatest compliment the Apostle Paul pays to the church in Rome is that their obedience is known by all.[8] Is obedience what our churches are known for? Is that what comes to mind when we think of our Christian friends or even ourselves? Surely we want to encourage both knowledge *and* obedience-based discipleship.

Obedience is giving the helm of the ship to God. It's allowing the obedient Christ to live in us and empower us to obey. It's something to learn, like a skill, over time. The Apostle Paul's plea to the young church in Thessalonica was, '*Finally, then, brothers, we ask and urge you in the Lord Jesus, that as you received from us how you ought to walk and to please God, just as you are doing, that you do so more and more.*' (1 Thessalonians. 4:1) In other words, they should devote their entire lives to increasing the skill of pleasing God through their obedience. It's his love language. It's how we demonstrate our devotion to Him.

The cost of disobedience

If we continue to avoid obedience, there will be implications for our walk with God and witness in the world. The cost of disobedience is paid by us and by non-Christians around us.

Just take our relationship with money and belongings. If we don't follow Jesus' way of generosity and simplicity, we will fail to escape the pull of consumerism and the burden of our competitive society. We will spend, borrow and consume to our hearts' content and miss the opportunity to be free from the inexhaustible drive to have more stuff. Without this freedom, we will probably suffer from the same sort of anxieties and levels of comparison that most people experience. We will fail to be radically different from the people around us, which in turn means we will lack an effective and distinctive witness among our neighbours.

Are we reinforcing disobedience?

Maybe our focus on Sunday attendance and teaching, coupled with a lack of feedback loops, often means we have a whole generation in the church trained in disobedience. We all love to feel challenged by a message and resonate with some new insight or see something that makes us sit up and take notice in the text, but none of that leads to a transformed life. Resonance isn't obedience. I would go as far as saying that preaching great sermons can make things both better *and* worse. I believe the Spirit uses faithful preaching to steadily feed us and draw us to Jesus. Yet, at the same time, it can train us to love knowledge or insight more than true conviction which always leads to repentance and life.[9] Maybe we, as church leaders, have unwittingly contributed to reinforcing intellectual learning over obedient living for Christ.

At Mosaic, we're on a journey of trying to balance expository teaching, that explains what the Bible is saying, with a focus on obediently working it out in our lives so that we're not unwittingly contributing to a passive, consumerist mindset. At one of our sites, we may break into smaller groups on a Sunday to discuss how the text in front of us applies to our lives, or leave space for people to think about what God is calling them to do in response to reading the Bible together. And the following Sunday, we ask whether we've done what we said we'd do. These feedback loops are not so much for checking up on each other as a way of underlining the importance of not only hearing God's word but obeying it.

A joyful loss of freedom

Obedience is a problematic word for many of us, because it infers a loss of freedom. Just as marriage involves a significant loss of freedom and autonomy, becoming a follower of Jesus means that we cannot simply live on our own terms. When a couple marry, they take on new obligations and duties, but gain the opportunity to experience love, acceptance and intimacy at a whole new level, along with a new sense of security and belonging, and because of this, the loss of freedom is a joy, not a burden. Going the extra mile becomes an expression of love, not an imposition. It's similar when we become followers of Jesus. We experience a new level of love, acceptance and intimate relationship with him, we have a new sense of security and belonging, and obedience becomes not a burden but a joy, as we seek the pleasure of pleasing God by curtailing our freedom and embracing obedience.

Going back to Isaiah's encounter with God, we can see that after the encounter and after the surrender came obedience. Isaiah has just received the scandalous mercy of having his guilt forgiven and his sin atoned for[10], when he hears the voice of God: *Then I heard the voice of the Lord saying, "Whom shall I send? And who will go for us?..."* (Isaiah 6:8) And his response is immediate: '*"Here am I. Send me!"'* (Isaiah 6:8)

If we've seen something of the glory of God, and realised how our sin and mess has cut us off from him, and if we've then tasted the glorious kindness and grace of God that forgives and sets us free – then our attitude inevitably shifts toward wanting to give everything in response. "*Here I am; use me.*"

And during my early years of being a Christian, that was my prayer, too. I was all in and determined to dedicate my life to whatever and wherever God wanted me. But I quickly found that obedience wasn't just for the big decisions in my life; it was about learning to hear God speak to the little things in life and doing exactly what he said. Of course, we all resist this voice.

Trust and obedience

Lars Due Christensen[11] tells this amusing tale of a man stuck on a cliff. '*Only his grip on a small, fragile tree prevented him from tumbling down into the rocky abyss. Desperate and scared, he looked up to the sky and shouted, "God, if you are there, please help me!" Immediately a voice from heaven replied, "Let go; I'll catch you." The man thought for a moment, and then cried, "Anybody else out there?"*' Lars says that our lives can sometimes feel like the man on the ledge, desperate enough to call out for help but not trusting God enough to let go.

Unsurprisingly obedience is related to faith and trust. In fact, the Greek word for '*obey*' in the New Testament (*hupakouo*) can also mean 'trust'.[12] Faith and obedience are two sides of the same coin. You cannot claim to have faith when there isn't any obedience in your life. You can tell a tree by its fruit. If there is no good fruit (obedience), there is no good tree (faith).[13]

The Bible also tells us that perfect faith is accompanied by action.[14] Obedience is the visible expression of invisible faith. We see this in the sad story of Adam and Eve's downfall in the garden. They fell for the serpent's lie that God didn't know best, and consequently disobeyed God's command not to eat from the tree. What about us? Do we trust God? Do we think of Jesus as the trustworthy holder of all knowledge and wisdom? Paul taught the early Christians to think of Jesus as one *"in whom are hidden all the treasures of wisdom and knowledge."* (Colossians 2:3 NAS) The greater our confidence and trust in God, the greater will be our obedience.

I saw this working out in Terry's life a few years ago. During his twenties he had racked up a large amount of debt from overspending on a luxurious lifestyle. He had bought cars, watches and jewellery, and gone on holidays to places he couldn't afford. Even though he was now a Christian and slowly paying off his debts, he couldn't bring himself to let go of his desire for famous clothing brands and the latest technology. He found his identity in being admired for his style and taste.

For Terry, the battle of obedience was a battle to trust that his identity in Christ held greater contentment and peace for him than the image he was trying to present to the world or the gadgets and clothes he wanted to buy. Obedience meant actively changing his mindset about his identity, rejecting the lifestyle he had adopted in the past and committing to daily simplicity. He found the change slow but ultimately liberating. By limiting his long held desires for popularity and expensive possessions, he discovered true freedom in trusting Jesus' acceptance and new priorities.

Love and obedience

Obedience is also related to love. How much do we trust that God loves us as his children? The more secure we are in our sonship, the more joyfully we will do what our heavenly Father says.

In his Gospel and letters, John links love for God with obedience to his commands more explicitly than any other biblical writer. He was convinced of this mutuality. The greater we know we are loved by God, the greater our own love for God. This in turn empowers our obedience to God (as we want to please

God and love the things he loves) and our love for our neighbour grows.[15] And it follows that if we don't love God first and foremost, we will be dissatisfied in our relationship with God and lack a desire to obey and therefore fall into disobedience.

Jesus describes these two potential outcomes- *'"If anyone loves Me, he will keep My word; and My Father will love him, and We will come to him and make Our home with him. He who does not love Me does not keep My words; and the word which you hear is not Mine but the Father's who sent Me."*[16] Love for God is an upward spiral that leads to greater obedience while love for things of the world, is a damaging, downward spiral into greater disobedience.

Joy and Obedience

Jesus illustrated the connection between obedience and joy in the parable he told in Matthew 13:44. *'The kingdom of heaven is like treasure hidden in a field. When a man found it, he hid it again, and then in his joy went and sold all he had and bought that field.'* The man had found something that brought him greater joy than anything else he owned, and *'in his joy'*, he did everything he could to gain the treasure of the kingdom.

Experiencing the greater satisfaction and joy of knowing a loving God provides us with the motivation to give up lesser joys and things that don't offer the same depth of satisfaction, and propels us towards a lifestyle of obedience to God, the great joy-giver.

Pastor John Piper describes this dynamic as *'Christian hedonism,'* which he defines as the conviction that God's ultimate goal in the world (his glory) and our deepest desire (to be happy) are one and the same, because God is most glorified in us when we are most satisfied in him.[17] The best way to remove a toy from the hands of a stroppy two-year-old is to offer a better toy. In a similar way, God offers us joy that is deeper, more satisfying and more long-lasting than anything the world can offer. And once we embrace it, we find we have a new eagerness to please God, and new desires to seek him in all of life. Our desires are relocated. We live increasingly to please him.

Obedience and the future

Lastly, obedience has an eschatological dimension, meaning we also look into the future for inspiration to be obedient in the present. We obey now in anticipation of a world where we will enjoy God's presence forever. We choose obedience, knowing we will be rewarded in the life to come.

Maybe you've had the experience of watching a trailer for an upcoming film, and by the end of it, you know enough to work out the basic plot line, what happens to the main characters and how the movie ends.

Similarly, as Christians, we can and should live in the light of what we know about how our story ends. We've seen the trailer - we know that Jesus defeated sin, death and the devil through his death and resurrection, and we know that the day will come when that victory is finally complete and we will join God in the new creation, where the presence of evil is gone forever and there's no more sin or suffering or death. The Apostle Peter asks what kind of people should we be becoming as we look forward to the new heavens and earth, and his answer is stunning. We're to be spotless, blameless, holy and godly.[18]

This means we follow the Apostle Paul's logic that if we *'set our minds on things above'*[19] our present suffering and difficulties become *'light and momentary as they are achieving for us an eternal glory that far outweighs them all'*.[20]

Our obedience and diligence seem to have eternal consequences in light of the resurrection. Every decision and action we make in this life becomes meaningful by the fact that, somehow, mysteriously, it has eternal significance and will be rewarded by God.[21] This is hugely motivating. It shifts our thinking from present and temporary to eternal and permanent. Hard, godly choices to put God first, difficult decisions to remain pure, patient and loving, and loving kindness towards undeserving people are all celebrated and rewarded in the new creation.[22]

Obedience is an action

Ultimately, obedience is an *action*, not a thought, attitude, or mindset. Obedience requires, by its very nature, a response towards what God asks of us. Obedience cannot be relegated to theory - obedience means we're actually *obeying* God.

So our question must be, do we want to live obedient lives? Do we desire to live for Jesus? Are we willing to ask the Spirit of God to strengthen our passion for obedience? If we can't answer positively yet, a helpful approach would be to ask what is holding us back. What are the things that stop us relinquishing control to God, and why do they have such a hold on us? Why is there such defiance in our hearts? Is there anything we're scared of losing? Do we imagine that God might suddenly force us to make decisions we couldn't live with?

Encouragingly, obedience is about taking things one step at a time. One obedience leads to another. We don't have to commit to everything all at once, but just to the next step of obedience. God is patient and kind. He will go at a pace we can manage and gently call us deeper into the discipleship journey.

It's helpful to keep this in mind, so that we don't imagine an obedient life is a perfect life where we never do anything wrong. A mindset like that may cause us to give up when we inevitably mess up! We can then easily become passive and unmotivated. Instead, a growing awareness of the kindness of God, coupled with the mindset that commits to one step at a time, and to having another go when we don't get it right first time, will enable us to persevere on the journey. And one day, however far we may think we still have to go, we'll look back and be amazed at how far we've come.

The reality is that no one lives in perfect obedience. No one is crushing the Christian life. In fact the closer we are to God the further away we may feel from him at times, as we become more sensitive to the things in our lives that don't please him. This is nothing to worry about - it's simply a normal part of our growth towards maturity.

Rather than being *perfectly* obedient we can try to be *truly* obedient. What I mean is that our posture needs to be submissive and humble as we try to obey God every day in the small things, yet acknowledge that our best efforts go hand in hand with failures. An obedient life is rarely spectacular. The beauty of obedience is that it's lived out in tiny, seemingly insignificant moments that accumulate into a life dripping with authority and integrity. In the moment, we may feel like we're failing, but over a lifetime those small acts of obedience lead to a life worthy of the calling we have received.

Summary

So there we have it - three characteristics that I've learnt are necessary to see lasting change in anyone. **Surrender, encounter and obedience**. The order in which we experience them doesn't matter. They aren't a set sequence of one-off experiences, but rather a cyclical process that keeps us humble, broken and available to God. Jesus emphasised these three things in his call to discipleship - *"'if you want to come after me (encounter) first deny yourself and take up your cross (surrender) and follow me (obedience).'"* (Luke 9:23) Our experience of discipling hundreds of people at Mosaic has been that lasting change only happens when these three things are present.

Spiritual formation requires true **surrender** and brokenness. Without it, people won't engage in God's mission; they won't even want to.

And if we don't **encounter** God's love and power through the Holy Spirit, we are left empty and lifeless. The Christian life becomes all about duty and trying really hard. God becomes distant, and all the power for godliness is lacking.

As we enter a life of surrender and encounter, a life of **obedience** naturally and typically emerges. This is simply the best life we could choose for anyone. God wants the best for us, so obedience to his Word can satisfy us like nothing else. We're designed to live this way.

I've seen these three traits exemplified in many people, including my friend Dave who became a Christian a few years ago. He works as a delivery driver and is married with three children. By his own admission, he struggles to spend much time with God, studying his Bible. He's not much of a reader, having dropped out of school without any qualifications, and he often feels he doesn't measure up to some of the expectations of the people around him. However, I see a life well lived. His childhood was very traumatic but he has given up many unhelpful habits that he picked up to cope with his past. He models surrender through daily decisions to not return to drinking and drug-taking. It's hard to fathom how challenging these choices are for him but he consistently resists the temptation to fall back into his old lifestyle.

His walk with God may look undisciplined and chaotic, but Dave talks to God all through his day delivering packages. He sings at the top of his voice in his van, making up his own songs and encountering God through worship and prayer.

I think he is radically obedient, though he can't see it himself. He often feels ashamed that he can't read the latest Christian book or pray elegant and sophisticated prayers. However, Dave loves people like no one else I know. You can't help but feel loved when you're in his presence. He always goes the extra mile to help out and as a result, there is a constant flow of people through their house. Lodgers, waifs and strays, people who want to chat, friends who come round to hang out. He particularly thrives when he gets time with people from underprivileged backgrounds. If maturity is measured in how much we love God and others, then Dave is a godly man of faith. He models for me the power of a life surrendered to God, with daily encounters with the Spirit and obedience to the commands of Jesus. Love comes so naturally to him. His transformation is inspirational because he reflects the heart of God so naturally.

Questions

1. Can you identify any ways in which you reinforce disobedience in your own life? Is there a way to break this pattern?

2. Try to remember a time where you obeyed God and it led to greater

love or joy. What things can you learn from this experience?

   3. What was the last thing you sensed God wanted you to do? Have you done it yet?

   4. What helps you obey God?

   5. Where do you most need to invest? In your surrender, encounter or obedience?

---

1. Matthew 28:20

2. John 14:23

3. Max Anders, 'Brave New Discipleship: Cultivating Scripture-Driven Christians in a Culture-Driven World' (Nashville, TN: Thomas Nelson, 2015), p.16.

4. Thanks to Jon Tyson, Church of the City, New York for the connection between the film 'A hidden life' and obeying God in unseen ways.

5. George Eliot ' Middlemarch' (Vintage Classics, 2007)

6. Kevin Deyoung 'The Hole in our holiness' (Crossway, 2012), p.19

7. (Matt 7:24-29, Philippians 4:9, James 1:22-27; 1 John 1:9-11)

8. Romans 16:19

9. 2 Cor 7:10

10. Isaiah 6:7

11. Lars Due Christensen, Steps course book, (Christ Church London publishing 2018) p. 28

12. There are at least five New Testament uses of 'hupakouo' that relate to obedience and trust/faith - Acts 6:7, Romans 6:17, Romans 10:16, 2 Thessalonians 1:8 and Hebrews 5:9

13. Matthew 7:17

14. James 2:14–26

15. John 13:34, 15:12, I John 3:23, 1 John 4:21, 2 John 5

16. John 14:23-24

17. John Piper, The Pleasures of God, Mentor Publishing, 2013

18. 2 Peter 3:11-14

19. Colossians 3:2

20. 2 Corinthians 4:7

21. James 1:12

22. Hebrews 10:34; 1 Timothy 6:18-19

For free discipleship resources and downloads, visit
www.matthatch.org

This includes an exclusive training video -
*'Three things holding back your transformation and
what you can do about them'*, downloadable PDFs,
and a 'How to start a Triplet' manual.

PART 2

DISCIPLESHIP PRINCIPLES AND TOOLS

Sequoia Tree Books

SEQUOIA TREE BOOKS

"Do not despair, thinking that you cannot change yourself after so many years. Simply enter into the presence of Jesus as you are and ask him to give you a fearless heart where he can be with you. You cannot make yourself different. Jesus came to give you a new heart, a new spirit, a new mind, and a new body. Let him transform you by his love and so enable you to receive his affection in your whole being."

Henri Nouwen
(Lent and Easter Wisdom)

SEVEN

WHO DO YOU THINK YOU ARE?

T his chapter is the launchpad for starting our discipleship journey. We've learnt about God's desire and commitment to make us more like Christ, and how this will require us to grow our surrender, encounter and obedience to him. We are now ready to start investing in our transformation by identifying three principles that will help us navigate the challenges ahead. The first is about *who* we think we are.

Identity

We often think the key to change is initiating new behaviours or habits. However, this is only one side of the equation. We also need to think about our self-perception -in other words, *who* we think we are. King Solomon, who was renowned for his wisdom, said, *"For as he thinks within himself, so he is."* (Proverbs 23:7a NASB) This means there is no chance of changing the way we live before we transform the way we think about ourselves. Or as James Clear, a change expert and the author of Atomic Habits, says, *"It's hard to change your habits if you never change the underlying belief that led you to your past behaviour. You have a new goal and a new plan, but you haven't changed who you are."*[1] In other words, your '*who*' always impacts your '*do*'.[2]

Where does self-identity come from?

All of us have an identity. It's how we find our way in the world. It's influenced by our heritage, family and ethnicity. Basically, anything we have or have gone without (such as wealth, success, social standing, and class) can impact how we see ourselves.

As Christians, sadly, we can have a view of ourselves that is rooted far more in how we or the world views us or what I have or do in life, rather than how the Bible defines us. Sometimes our identity is found in the things we struggle with. "I am depressed", "I am alone", "I am a failure", "I am an addict".

Social media has further complicated things by allowing us to present ourselves digitally to those who don't know us. Our increasingly self-curated identities mean we can be whatever we want it to be. We can reveal the side of ourselves we want others to see and conceal those aspects of our lives we want to hide.

Mark Zuckerberg, the founder of Facebook, openly admits this, '*Think about what people are doing on Facebook today. They're keeping up with their friends and family, but they're also building an image and identity for themselves, which in a sense is their brand. They're connecting with the audience that they want to connect to. It's almost a disadvantage if you're not on it now.*' [3] In addition to this, the internet provides access to an endless supply of influential voices that impact our view of self. It's unsurprising that many of us are confused about who we are.

It's not really about the hair clips

Many of us also need help identifying the lies we believe about ourselves. These lies are often at the root of a wrong self-identity. I remember hearing of a young, newly married couple in our church struggling to live together for the first time. The husband had a particular gripe with his wife's habit of leaving hair clips around the house. He'd find them on the sofa, in the bathroom, on the bed, on the floor, in fact, everywhere he looked, there they were!

Sadly, his constant frustration boiled over into constantly lecturing his wife. I took him to one side and said, *'Look, mate, you are vastly overreacting to this; what's really going on?'* He defended himself and said he couldn't tolerate her wanton hair clip dropping, which needed addressing and so I pushed further and asked why it drove him crazy. He struggled to answer but did admit he was a little OCD about things like this and thrived when his house was clean and tidy.

Now, it would be easy to leave it there and simply say, *'Come on, fella, get a life, pick your battles, either let it go or buy her a box to keep them in.'* But it would miss the heart and this discipleship moment. So I asked again, *'Why is this such a big deal?'* He reluctantly admitted he wanted everyone to think they were clean and tidy people. I probed further, *'Why do you think like that?'* He said, *'My Mum always taught us to make sure we presented our house in perfect order to others'.* *'In fact'*, he said, *'I remember visiting someone's house that was way messier than ours and my mum spoke harshly about them in the car on the way home and condemned them for being so untidy'.*

So, again I said, *'What's really happening with the hair clips?'* In a moment of inspiration, he said, *'I don't want people to judge us or look down on us because our house is untidy.'* *'Oh,'* I replied, *'so what is the real issue here?'* The young man replied (sheepishly) *'Ohh, it's about being secure in my identity in Christ and not worrying what other people think'* We had hit the root issue. We'd found the lie he was believing that brought about his extreme reaction. With this knowledge, we could go to work. His behaviour and interaction with his wife could change as he rejected lies about his identity being dependent on other people thinking well of him, and started to believe in his true identity in Christ.

Defining Identity

So, how do we view ourselves? I've found it helpful to think about the late Henri Nouwen's description of the five lies of identity we tend to succumb to.[4]

1) I am what I have.

2) I am what I do.

3) I am what other people say or think of me.

4) I am nothing more than my worst moment.

5) I am nothing less than my best moment.

6) I am what I feel.

I've added the sixth lie, '*I am what I feel,*' which is not part of Nouwen's list, because I think it's important to recognise the power of our emotions in determining who we think we are.

'In Christ'

In contrast, The New Testament authors are clear that our true identity is found in none of these things, but in Christ. They do not hold back when they describe our blessings in Christ, using words like 'lavish', 'riches', 'wealth', 'indescribable', and 'surpassing greatness'. Such extravagant language points to a new identity almost too good to be true.[5]

The Apostle Paul's constant desire is for Christians to receive revelation by the Holy Spirit of everything that is already theirs in Christ. He taught that the moment we respond to God's invitation, we die, are buried and are now raised with Christ.[6] We have been given new life with new desires in a new community. 1 John 3:9 tells us, '*No one who is born of God will continue to sin, because God's seed remains in him; he cannot go on sinning, because he has been born of God.*' We have been given new spiritual DNA, a new start and a new nature. We're no longer in Adam, who set the pattern of human disobedience and sin which we're unable to escape from by our own efforts, but are now in Christ, whose righteousness and obedience has set us free to live righteous and obedient lives in him.[7] Gloriously, our identity is received not achieved.

Power over the law, sin, and death.

What is more, the spoils of victory, earned by Christ's atoning death and demonstrated in his resurrection, mean that in him we have power over the worst the enemy can throw at us. In the words of Thabiti Anyabwile, *'Jesus died. Death is destroyed. Satan, the one who holds the power of death, is destroyed. Death and sin no longer have mastery. Death cannot separate us from the love of God. This is why the gospel, when it is properly understood, floods a man with such delight and boldness in the face of death. This is why Paul almost sings: "Where, O death, is your victory? Where, O death, is your sting?"*[8] We are free. We are no longer slaves to sin. The power of sin that had us in chains is now thoroughly beaten and humiliated. Sin's impact is not destroyed, but it is defeated. The cross is ground zero in the battle against sin and its effect in our lives.

I often imagine myself on the upper deck of an open-top bus that's making its way along a street lined with fans. But we're not a football team celebrating a great win. This celebration is about Jesus, who's there on the top of the bus, holding aloft not the FA Cup or even the World Cup trophy, but a cross-shaped trophy that symbolises the defeat of everything that opposed God. The crowds are cheering and celebrating this victory of victories, while our defeated enemies are being jeered and laughed at. And somehow, I'm on top of that bus, too. Somehow, Jesus' victory is also my victory. The overflow of Jesus' life, death and resurrection apply to me as if I was the one winning the most important contest in history. I get to hold the cup above my head and celebrate the win. I hope you can see yourself doing the same.[9]

This means there is no habitual sin that is impossible to overcome, and no pain so great that the Comforter can't soothe it. We are not what our parents thought of us. We are not bound by our cultural background, class or body type. We are not what people have called us in the past, and our mistakes, past and future, do not define us. Our identity in Christ trumps all of them. It doesn't mean we lose ourselves or our heritage; it simply means our identity in Christ becomes the first and foremost way in which we see ourselves. This is who we really are.

How to change?

So how do we change lifelong thinking about ourselves? How do we draw down on our status in Christ in this life? The way we have always thought about ourselves becomes strongly ingrained in our thinking, like a muddy track that a tractor has driven over for so long that ruts have formed. With every passing season, the ruts have deepened, making it impossible to turn out of them and choose a different route. Changing the way we see ourselves is like trying to turn the wheel and steer out of the ruts; each time we think we're out, the wheels slide back into the old ruts and real change seems impossible.

The good news is, however, that with God nothing is impossible! Though it may take time and effort on our part. Change starts with recognising that we have a new identity and new life in Christ - as Paul explains in 2 Corinthians 5:17, *'if anyone is in Christ, they are a new creation; the old has gone, the new has come.'* Armed with this truth, we can begin to reject our old, unsaved identity, which is no longer true of us. This work is called the renewing of our minds.

The Apostle Paul instructs us, *'Do not conform to the pattern of this world, but be transformed by the renewing of your mind. Then you will be able to test and approve what God's will is—his good, pleasing and perfect will.'* (Romans 12.1–2) Paul uses the word *'transformed'* to describe how fundamental and far-reaching this process of sanctification is. The Greek word for transformation is *'metamorphoo'* from which we get the word metamorphosis. It's the same word Matthew and Mark use to describe how Jesus is changed at the transfiguration. Think of a tadpole turning into a frog, or a caterpillar into a butterfly. Paul is saying, *'be metamorphosed by the renewing of your mind.'* It's the overriding passion of this book. Wholesale change is possible in Christ.[10]

Theologian Richard Longnecker emphasises the implications of this for every aspect of our lives. *'This remarkable 'metamorphosis' that Paul speaks of here is not some pattern of external decorum or form of outward expression that believers in Jesus are to accept by way of a makeover of their lives and practices. Rather it is a complete inner change of thought, will and desires that Christians are to allow God by means of the ministry of his Holy Spirit to bring about in their lives, resulting in a recognisable external change of actions and of conduct.*[11]

This means there is a genuine interplay between our transformation and the renewal of our minds. Experiencing a metamorphosis into Christlikeness depends on our pursuit of renewal in our thinking. This is why immature Christians can outwardly look like disciples of Jesus, but inside they're dominated by anxiety, anger, lust or fear. They've not invested in their '*who*'.

How to Practise renewing our minds

The renewal of our minds is not a quick fix, but is likely to be a long-term project and an all-out battle. If we've spent years believing things about ourselves that are no longer true, it's likely to take a long time to undo all the lies we've believed and the scripts we've created. (By 'script' I mean a fixed series of behaviours we follow, often unconsciously, in certain situations.)

I read recently about a lady called Teri Horton, who lived in California. She retired from truck driving after an accident, and spent her time hunting for bargain treasures. In 1992, she stumbled across a large abstract painting that she bought for $5 in a thrift store. After being tipped off by a local art teacher, she took the painting to experts who confirmed it was an authentic Jackson Pollock. (A similar work sold for $140 million in 2006.) Teri didn't actually like the painting but upon hearing its potential value, she refused to sell unless she got a price close to the valuation. Even though she was broke, she turned down an offer of $2 million and later an offer of $9 million, insisting the painting was worth more. She died in 2018, still holding onto the painting and never cashing in on her remarkable find.

For Christians, renewing our mind is an exercise in claiming what is already ours in Christ. It's no use, like Teri, simply knowing about the benefits and privileges of our new status. We need to 'cash them in', we need to apply these truths to ourselves rather than hold on to them and hope that somehow, they will impact our lives just because we know about them.

Renewing our minds involves an exchange. We eject wrongful thinking in exchange for truth. American Bible teacher Beth Moore once asked, *"What's the knot in your rope?"*[12] In other words, what do you hold onto when it feels like you're sliding down the rope into wrong thinking, palms burning and blistering?

I've found it helpful to hold onto specific biblical truths when my mind or emotions are causing me to freefall into old thinking about my identity. I actively command (sometimes out loud) my thoughts to fall in line with my new reality. I once wrote out some Bible verses and put them in my shower to repeat to myself each morning. Other times I've had them on index cards that I've carried around with me. You may find more creative ways to do this, but the goal is to focus on these truths every day and claim them for yourself.[13]

Use these wonderful truths to fight against the identity lies (false self) you may face:

John 1:12

False self: Spiritual Orphan

New self: child of God

1 Peter 2:4-6

False Self: isolated individual

New Self: Family member

Romans 6:18

False self: slaves to sin

New self: slaves of righteousness

1 Peter 1:8

False self: haters of God

New self: lovers of God

Colossians 2:13

False self: spiritually dead

New self: spiritually alive

Romans 8:35-39

False self: powerless against Satan

New self: victorious against Satan

1 Corinthians 6:11

False self - Idolators

New Self - Worshippers

Step in - Step out

One way we have helped people think about the battle for the mind is by using a guide called 'Step in - Step out'.

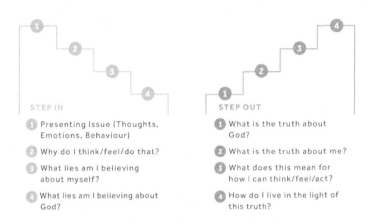

STEP IN

1. Presenting Issue (Thoughts, Emotions, Behaviour)
2. Why do I think/feel/do that?
3. What lies am I believing about myself?
4. What lies am I believing about God?

STEP OUT

1. What is the truth about God?
2. What is the truth about me?
3. What does this mean for how I can think/feel/act?
4. How do I live in the light of this truth?

It's a simple way to link our presenting issues and feelings with the lies we believe about ourselves and God. From that place, we can remind ourselves of the truth about God, our identity in Christ and let this renew our thoughts, feelings and actions.

For example, my friend Phil is a brilliant church leader. He excels in preaching, leading worship and hosting meetings. He's also a fantastic mimic, quick-witted, regularly making people laugh out loud. However, he's fairly uncomfortable around people and often assumes that people don't like him. This makes him fairly reserved around new people. He has historically struggled to make deep friendships and often feels misunderstood and unknown. How could we help him unearth the untruths that need identifying, removing and replacing? Here's what we discovered when doing the step-in, step-out exercise.

Step-in

1) What is the presenting issue?

Phil's presenting issues are that he feels alone and incapable of friendship, while what everyone else sees is a very talented and gifted leader. He sometimes gives the impression that he's not interested in spending time with others, while inside he desperately wants to. He feels uncomfortable in groups and often avoids situations where he has to spend a long time with people. He doesn't acknowledge his feelings or let other people see them.

2) Why do I feel and behave like this?

Phil is like this because he doesn't think people are interested in him. Growing up, he was distant from his mum and dad who, although they loved and cared for him, always kept their distance emotionally. His dad never showed any emotion apart from anger. Phil struggles with intimacy because no one showed him how to do it in a safe way. He struggles with acceptance because his family prized performance and achievement over unconditional love.

3) What lies am I believing about myself?

Phil believes that he doesn't have what it takes to be a great friend. He doesn't believe people can like him for who he is, only for what he does and is successful at. He doesn't think he can open up and be vulnerable.

4) What lies am I believing about God?

Phil doesn't believe fully that God loves him unconditionally.

Step out

1) What is the truth about God?

Phil needs to know that God is a father who loves him no matter what his performance or achievements are, and that this love can be tangibly experienced through the Holy Spirit.[14]

2) What is the truth about me?

The truth about Phil is that he is worthy and capable of friendship because of who God has made him to be. It's not dependent on his gifts or performance. His security and confidence can grow because they aren't based on how people feel about him but reliant on who he is in Christ.

3) What does this mean for how I can think/feel/act?

This means that Phil can grow in being vulnerable and intimate with others. He doesn't need to assume that people don't like him or are uninterested in him. He can feel safe and at ease when talking about his emotions.

4) How do I live in the light of this truth?

In his turn, Phil will consciously look to be open with his feelings when asked about them. He will be proactive in making and deepening friendships with others. He will work at becoming more aware of how his behaviour pushes people away, and changing those behaviours.

Knowing ourselves and the unruly thoughts that fly around our minds may help us understand why we behave in certain ways or have persistent, sinful habits. 'Step in, - step out' helps diagnose the problem and has the potential to lead us into the truth and freedom.

For a free PDF of 'Step in -Step out' visit www.matthatch.org

Be Ruthless

Lastly, let me warn you what we're up against when we try to renew our minds. Before we became Christians, we didn't acknowledge God and our minds were given over to do what we ought not to do.[15] Our desire to live without God meant that God gave us over to our sinful desires, and these desires left us ignorant and blind to the things of God. We might not have realised it or consciously chosen this status, but the Bible explains that we were hard-hearted and enemies of God in our minds.[16] This changed instantaneously when God, in his grace, welcomed us into his kingdom.

No wonder we're on a long journey of renewal! It's not surprising there are all kinds of things that cloud our minds and clutter our thoughts. No wonder wrong thinking and areas of weakness permeate our minds. God, however, wants to set us free from the lust, anxiety, greed, envy, or fear that infects or dominates our lives. These things don't just disappear when we're saved, rather we fight them with newfound freedom and power to change. Our minds have been occupied by the enemy and now we need to take back that space.

This means we need to avoid or tread carefully around people or places that lead our minds astray. Just as a reformed alcoholic will change their friends, habits, and the places they go, in order to avoid temptation, so we need to ruthlessly eliminate these options until we're strong enough to resist. For some of us, renewing our minds means finding new ways to pursue purity. We need mental discipline to focus on whatever is true and pure rather than our old patterns of sinful thinking.[17] We need to be alive to the temptation to reject what the Bible says about our status and identity.

Your *who* impacts your *do*. Fight for the renewal of your mind and your status in Christ and it will set a foundation for seeing God transform your life.

Questions:

1. Consider how you see yourself. Are there any lies you believe about yourself? Who has shaped your view of yourself the most?

2. Can you identify and then renounce the lies about your true identity in Christ? What biblical truths do you need to fight against these untruths? How might the 'Step in - Step out' method help you navigate through your thoughts and feelings?

3. What does it look like for you to fight intentionally against old ways of thinking? Are there situations or people that you need to avoid for a season?

---

1. James Clear, Atomic Habits: An Easy and Proven Way to Build Good Habits and Break Bad Ones (New York: Penguin Random House, 2018), p.33.

2. This idea is taken from Craig Groeschel, The Power to Change. (Zondervan 2023). Kindle Edition. p. 13

3. Mark Zuckerberg, The Wired Interview https://www.wired.com/2009/06/mark-zuckerberg-speaks/

4. Henri J. M. Nouwen, 'Who Are We?' (Ave Maria Press, 2006)

5. Inspired by a tweet from Terry Virgo 6:15 AM · Apr 5, 2023

6. Romans 6:3-4

7. Romans 5:12-15

8. Thabiti Anyabwile, Council member of The Gospel Coalition, Article in Gospel Coalition website, April 2015 https: //www.thegospelcoalition.org/blogs/thabiti-anyabwile/ the-death-of-death-in-the-death-of-christ-means-victory-over-death-for-those-who-believe/

9. Colossians 2:11-15

10. Matthew 17:2; Mark 9:2

11. Longenecker, R. N. The Epistle to the Romans, NIGTC, (Grand Rapids: Eerdmans 2016) p.923

12. Beth Moore. Tweet

13. 2 Corinthians 10:5-6

14. Romans 5:5

15. Romans 1:21-32; 2 Corinthian 4:3-4

16. Ephesians 2:1-3

17. Philippians 4:8

"You don't realize your story is changing you
until you look back."

Donald Miller
(A Million Miles in a Thousand Years)

EIGHT

LOOKING BACK TO LOOK FORWARD

I'm not a natural at home improvement. Most things I fix quickly need fixing again. Despite these failings, I decided to redecorate our downstairs bathroom. I wanted to do a good job, so I prepared all the walls for painting and chose a great colour by myself. I sanded all the wood, primed and painted it. I even removed some tiles from around the sink and re-laid some new subway tiles all by myself.

Things were looking good till I came to the last job. I needed to put some fancy handles on the vanity unit under the basin. The new handles were 'C' shaped and required two holes for their screws. The door already had a single hole, so I measured the top half of the new handle to this hole and drew around the bottom of the handle so I knew where to drill the new hole. I diligently drilled the hole, but when I came to screw in the handle, it didn't fit into the new hole! It was in the wrong place. *'Okay, I thought, that's not great, but I have another door to try.'* So I repeated the process, but this time triple measured to get the new hole in the right place. I even used a spirit level to get it bang on. However, once again, when I tried to fit the new 'C' shaped handle, it didn't fit. All that effort and I had four random holes in my cabinet.

I'm embarrassed to report that I was so devastated, I sat on my toilet facing the ruined cupboard for fifteen minutes. Whenever someone sat on this toilet,

I thought, they would see how rubbish I was at home improvement. I got so worked up that I let out a long agonising cry of frustration.

My wife quickly appeared at the door and, having experienced many of my failed home improvement projects, gave me that look which said, '*What have you done now?*' I told her (in not so many words) to leave me alone and continued to fume. I couldn't help but think, '*I have ruined the whole project; what would people think? This is what I always do. At some point, I always get it totally wrong.*' And from nowhere, suddenly, I thought, '*I've not just made a mistake; I am a mistake.*'

It was a window into my heart and a clear discipleship moment. Why was I so concerned with what everyone thought of me (and my house) and how did that link so closely with my sense of worth? On the surface, I had simply drilled some holes incorrectly, but deeper down was a desperation to impress others, a deep sense of shame, and a tendency to set myself unreasonably high standards. Why couldn't I engage in some DIY without it becoming such a difficult and exposing experience?

Looking back to go forward

The answer lay in my history. For many years, I was totally unaware of how my past impacted my present and future. Like many people, I chose to bury or minimise my past without realising how much it negatively affected my life. We can fear unhealthy introspection or navel-gazing, or it can even feel we're not being true to our new nature by rummaging around in the past. If we're Christians, we may have been told many times that '*the old has gone, the new has come,*' (2 Corinthians 5:17) and therefore, it's only the present that counts.

But we have to go backwards before we can go forwards. Yes, there may be trauma in our lives that will need to be unpacked and processed with great care, and this may seem daunting, but ignoring it doesn't make it go away. The philosopher Socrates was a tad more brutal in his assessment of people who don't look to their past - "*The unexamined life is not worth living.*"

I had assumed that what was in the past stayed in the past, but it doesn't. Only now do I realise how deeply the pain of rejection cut into my life. As I look back on my early life, I realise that nearly every significant person rejected me in different ways, which left me with a huge, gaping need to be accepted by others. And very early on, I developed complex coping mechanisms to help me get what I needed. This meant that I was fearful, emotionally withdrawn, focused on externals and caught between being desperate to succeed and tremendously fearful of trying and failing. My desire to succeed in doing simple home improvements had a dark side - an unacknowledged need to build a home that made me look more acceptable to other people.

It would be naive to think I'm immune from these traumatic moments. God does change our status and standing before him when we're saved, but we are still essentially '*us*.' This includes all the impact of our past, our family of origin and our upbringing, which all come to bear on how we live in the present. As author Pete Scazzero quips, *Jesus may be in your heart, but grandpa is in your bones. And the task of discipleship is to get Jesus more and more into your bones.*[1]

The influences that shape us

Authors Randy Reese and Robert Loane took distinguished researcher Robert Clinton's groundbreaking work on biblical and contemporary Christian leadership and brought it up to date in their book 'Deep Mentoring'.[2] They suggest how critical it is for a leader to understand the shaping influences of the past on their values, personality, decision making and skill sets. They termed it '*the foundational phase*'. It covers childhood to young adulthood.

In this phase, our natural default mechanisms or habits of managing life become instilled through things such as our family of origin, social influences, historical context (when and where we grew up) and spiritual background (Christian, backslidden, or non-Christian). These foundational things, which we have no control over, play a major role in making us who we are.

For example, I'm very grateful for my father's passion for sports, sense of humour and leadership. I've inherited those things from him and from being around him. I had no control over them, but they have significantly shaped my working and recreational life, mainly for good.

My mother is a caring, people-centred person. Her role leading the team in the Intensive Care Unit at the hospital made her unflappable and appealed to her inner passion for bringing healing to others. I've inherited this from her and absorbed it from growing up around it. Much of my interest in people and their growth is from her. I marvel at God's wisdom in placing me in my family. It's been a joy to recognise and invest in these strengths and be thankful for them. Recognising them has given me great confidence in God's goodness and sovereignty, even over the most painful parts of my story.

However, alongside these positive attributes, we can inherit some negative ones. Perhaps our family was never good with money, or there were patterns of addictive behaviour, or emotions were discouraged or never expressed. I've met many men who think they are emotionally repressed, but the truth is that their dads never expressed their own feelings in a healthy way, so their sons never learnt to do so either.

All this leaves us with specific patterns of thought and behaviour that we repeat from generation to generation, and which need to be brought under the lordship of Christ. The point is that these influences (good and bad) need recognising and then holding up against the example of Jesus and the truth of scripture.

All these things, in turn, influence our values, our internal coping systems and our ability to mature and grow. Therefore, if we can understand our roots and past, we can recover from them or leverage them for greater effectiveness. Alongside understanding the shaping influences in our lives, we must also deal with the more traumatic or difficult parts of our stories.

Simply put, if we are unaware of what is really going on internally, then we can't offer it to God for transformation. An unresolved past will be chock full of hurts, wounding, unforgiveness, coping mechanisms, and defence mechanisms that need to be processed through the cross.

Many years ago, I remember chatting with a friend who had been a church leader for around ten years. Though she had served her church faithfully and was a gifted communicator, she had never felt she had permission to talk about her past with anyone except her husband. So she hid it. She ignored it. And silently and steadily, the secret she had buried grew and grew. Or rather, the shame she felt grew. And the longer she left it, the greater the weight of guilt, and the more she worried that someone would find out at some point. She constantly feared it would disqualify her from ministry and she would lose everything.

Simply by providing a safe place for her to talk (by sharing all of the skeletons in my closet first), we enabled her to feel ready to reveal her big secret to our little discipleship group. With tears and tremendous courage, she explained that she fell pregnant in her late teens, and her baby was adopted by another family. You could physically see the weight of remorse and shame drop off of her as we listened, prayed and reminded her gently of Jesus' forgiveness and power to restore honour.

This engagement with her past had enormous consequences for her present and future. She was suddenly free to live without the nagging shame that had dogged her. She started to lead with new confidence in her integrity. She even found new levels of empathy with those who struggled to share their own past. By unlocking her past, her eyes were opened to the grace of God and how God wanted to redeem her life.

Telling your story

God loves to take the most broken parts of our lives, redeem them and then use them to form a central part of your ministry and testimony of his goodness towards you. God can rescue times of failure, questioning, hurt, rebellion, pain, loss and suffering. But it will require the hard work of breaking the power of the past - going back before you can go forwards.

To facilitate breaking the power of the past, I encourage people to tell their stories (after they've heard mine) in the safety of a small, trusted group. This enables them to understand life isn't a series of unrelated events but rather a journey that God is shaping and using for his glory.

One way to view our life is as a film with a storyline. Until we retell our story, we can feel as if the storyline is sweeping us along, and that life just happens to us. We can find ourselves living with the consequences of decisions we never knew we were making. Without self-knowledge, we end up being a particular sort of person without consciously realising or intending to.

Standing back and framing the narrative of our life means we can start to understand and even have some authority over it. This change from actor to co-author of our own story is empowering and in time, this self-knowledge leads to a greater knowledge of God and his work in our lives.[3]

Spiritual health comes from knowing our story. This helps us understand our motives, experiences, reactions, coping mechanisms, struggles and strongholds and places us in a humble posture of weakness and vulnerability. It allows us to open our hearts to God's healing power and the power of biblical truths.

Throughout the Old Testament, God reminded the Israelites of their story, particularly of those critical moments where they had either abandoned him or obeyed him. God regularly asked the Israelites to remember his working on their behalf, to reflect on the journey so far, and to step into his purposes. *'Remember that you were slaves in Egypt and that the Lord your God brought you out of there with a mighty hand and an outstretched arm. Therefore the Lord your God has commanded you to observe the Sabbath day.'* (Deuteronomy 5:15) And again in Deuteronomy 7:18, *'But do not be afraid of them; remember well what the Lord your God did to Pharaoh and to all Egypt'.*

Alongside remembering, God wanted his people to examine their own motives and actions more deeply. Lamentations 3:40 captures the heart of this: *'Let us examine our ways and test them, and let us return to the Lord.'*

In the New Testament, too, there are frequent calls to look inside and go beyond the surface layers of our actions. Paul instructs the Corinthians to check their attitude toward one another before taking communion, by examining their hearts: *'Let a person examine himself, then, and so eat of the bread and drink of the cup,'* (1 Corinthians 11:28). And again to the Corinthians, *'Examine yourselves to see whether you are in the faith; test yourselves. Do you not realise that Christ Jesus is in you – unless, of course, you fail the test?'* (2 Corinthians 13:5)

We're not to stumble blindly from one thing to the next. We're encouraged by various biblical authors to look back and consider the state of our lives and our need for Christ.[4] We're to take into consideration our history, fight the good fight of faith in the present and to anticipate and contemplate our future resurrection and eternity in the new heaven and earth.[5] All this means that transformational discipleship involves paying attention to the past, the present and the future, but we often forgo examining the past because of the demands of the here and now.

Self-examination

Why is looking back such a big deal? At Mosaic, we've found that telling your story helps you pay attention to how God has shaped us and shown up in our lives. It enables us to grow in understanding him as we're reminded of his actions in our lives.

Storytelling allows us to step back and examine why we acted as we did. This bigger picture of understanding our story and God's work in our lives helps us discover the things that hinder or help our formation. Rich Villodas reminds us why it's worth spending time on our story: '*The goal of self-examination is freedom—freedom from destructive thought patterns, inner messages, and the ways we wrongly perceive things.*'[6]

Telling our story will reveal key relationships and how they've shaped us, starting with our relationships, or our lack of connection, with parents and carers. Often it will show us how God was at work behind the scenes, drawing us to himself before we were aware of it. And it will begin to expose unhelpful coping mechanisms and lies we have believed about God and the gospel.

Telling our story can reveal strongholds where our wrong thinking and wrong behaviour have made us vulnerable to spiritual attack. It will also unearth some hidden treasures, those moments when we were unaware God was quietly working behind the scenes.

Telling our story only works if we're willing to think about *every* area of our life, even the most shameful, painful parts. This may require some specialised help and great care, but there is much that can be talked about in a safe and confidential environment. Doing this will no doubt lead us to areas of trauma and pain, but talking about these, instead of continuing to conceal or ignore them, opens us to the possibility that God wants to bring forgiveness and healing to rejection, shame, guilt, and grief. Wisdom and common sense are needed here, but I believe many of us would benefit from processing our past experiences with trusted disciplers.

If we choose to hide or ignore the pain we carry, and never look closely at our lives, it usually means that our past hurts, traumas and challenges are never truly dealt with and can end up seeping out into our lives in the form of anger, scapegoating, judgment and bitterness. As Richard Rhor helpfully says, *'If we do not transform our pain, we will most assuredly transmit it—usually to those closest to us: our family, our neighbors, our co-workers, and, invariably, the most vulnerable, our children.'*[7] The reason we find some sinful attitudes or habits so hard to break in the present is that they were often formed in our early years. It takes the hard work of processing these critical moments with God and allowing the Holy Spirit to bring restoration, forgiveness and freedom.

How to tell your story?

The storytelling I'm referring to is more than just a chronology of events; an account of what we've achieved in life, how many qualifications we've got, or where we've travelled. It's not even focused on how we became Christians. In other words, this is more than just about the facts and figures of our lives. Instead, we're looking for the *critical moments* of our life, the moments that have shaped us positively and negatively. This isn't just about raking over the ashes of past mistakes, but a chance to see God's work in our lives and the impact of past sins or victories over sin. It gives room to talk about where we've been sinned against or suffered injustice.

Our experience at Mosaic suggests that telling our story in this way takes several attempts among people who know us well and can speak the truth in love to help us understand how our past impacts our present. Most of us need feedback and active listening to help us unpack what was happening and what we truly felt in those critical moments. I've told my story hundreds of times, and each time I tell it, I learn, adjust and peel back another layer of revelation in self-understanding.

One way to start is to write down everything you can remember from your life on Post-it notes and then put them in chronological order. You may even want to use different coloured notes to show positive or negative experiences. This, too, may require several attempts. As the picture of your life builds up, you can discern different chapters or stages of your life that will help structure its retelling. Crucially, the negative, critical moments are most important in self-discovery. Here are my 'chapters' from telling my story.

Chapters	Critical moments	Significance/feelings
Parents' divorce	Dad left	Rejection
Mum remarries	Step-dad arrives	Double rejection/crushed
Teenage years	Christian & backsliding	Calling into ministry, fear and shame. Dealing with sin
Uni	Compromise, filled with Spirit, discipled	Surrender, Encounter, Obedience
Ministry	Leadership growth	Deconstruction of faith
Marriage	Living with Pip	Forgiveness and Loving patience
Leeds	Work in call centre	Identity, Jesus not ministry
Mosaic	Planting and establishing	Gifts and passions
Counselling	Confessing my issues	Feeling stuck, body image and rejection
Sabbatical	Emotionally tired	Surrender and repentance
Turning 50	Multiplication and legacy	At peace with myself & calling

Finding someone who can provide a safe, listening environment in which you can piece together your story is crucial. At Mosaic, we run short-term discipleship groups of up to four people who take turns telling their stories. One of these people is a leader who tells their story first and helps others learn how to tell theirs. In every group we run, we emphasise the need for confidentiality to create a safe environment for people to talk. However, we encourage married group members to share their stories with their spouses.

More than just listening.

The vital part of these groups is that they are more than just listening to people's past. We take the difficult things or critical moments and bring them to God. We ask if there are ways of coping or lies we believe that don't match the truth about God or the gospel. We look at where we need to repent or forgive others. We look at sinful patterns of thinking or habitual sin and try to determine why we were drawn to them. This helps identify where our actual fight for freedom and holiness can begin. We support and encourage each other to follow Christ and imitate his life. So let me be clear, knowing your story is the first step towards transformation. The point is that we bring this new self-awareness to God and he is the one who can heal us.

Questions

1. Have you ever thought about how your background impacts your Christian life today? How do you feel about looking backwards to go forwards?

2. Why not make a start on piecing together your own story? Start by writing out all the critical moments (good and bad) you can think of.

3. Arrange them in chronological order and see if you can group any of them together into 'chapters'.

4. Write down how those critical moments made you feel and why you think they may be significant.

5. Return to this in a few days time and add to your story. Take some time to ask the Holy Spirit to reveal the significance of some of these events and how they might affect you today.

6. Is there a trusted friend you could do this activity with?

1. Pete Scazzero, tweet 8:05 PM · Jun 30, 2017

2. Randy D Reese and Robert Loane, 'Deep Mentoring: Guiding Others on Their Leadership Journey', (Intervarsity Press, 2012)

3. Augustine famously said 'Grant Lord that I may know myself that I may know thee". Self-knowledge and God-knowledge go hand in hand.

4. 1 Corinthians 1:26

5. Ephesians 1:3-14; 1 Peter 1:13

6. Rich Villodas, 'The Deeply Formed Life' (The Crown Publishing Group. Kindle Edition.) p.151

7. Richard Rohr, Transforming Pain, Online Article, 17th October, 2018. https://cac.org/daily-meditations/transforming-pain-2018-10-17/

"Everyone is in a process of spiritual formation! Every thought we hold, every decision we make, every action we take, every emotion we allow to shape our behaviour, every response we make to the world around us, every relationship we enter into, every reaction we have towards the things that surround us and impinge on our lives - all these things, little by little, are shaping us into some kind of being. We are being shaped into either the wholeness of the image of Christ or a horribly destructive caricature of that image - destructive not only to ourselves but also to others, for we inflict our brokenness upon them."

Robert Mulholland Jr
(Invitation to a Journey)

NINE

THE CHANGE CIRCLE

M any years ago, we moved into a house nearer our children's school. The place was great, and the neighbourhood delightful, yet devastatingly, after about a month, we discovered our neighbours hated us. They harboured an active hostility that manifested itself at every opportunity. To this day we have no idea what we did to offend them, but they made it clear we were unwelcome. They would bang on the walls, swear, and rage if they thought we made too much noise. They would come over from time to time to vent their anger over the pettiest things.

All this meant our home became a tense and horrible place to live. My heart sank as I rounded the corner on my way home and saw their car in the drive, signifying they were at home. I thought to myself, '*We were nice, lovable people - why have they taken such a dislike to us? What on earth did we do wrong?*'

We laid hands on our connecting wall in our better moments and prayed our hearts out. Members of the church came around to pray for them and us. We tried to reach out to them, talk and apologise. However, on my worst days, I daydreamed about doing things to them that I am too ashamed to write down. I was angry and wanted revenge for the way they had made life so difficult for us.

This was, of course, a *discipleship moment*. God hadn't left us to figure this out for ourselves; instead, he wanted to redeem this moment for our good. I wonder how other Christians might start to disciple me in this situation. Maybe they'd try to figure out how I could fix things or what I could do to make amends. Maybe they'd tell me to forgive my neighbours daily, or to consider moving house! These are all excellent ideas but probably won't get to the heart of the problem.

If we are to have churches that produce disciples, everyone needs to know how God transforms our lives in these moments. Awareness is often half the battle, so this chapter looks at a tool to help us understand *why* we are reacting in the way we are and *what* we should do to experience transformation.

The Change Circle

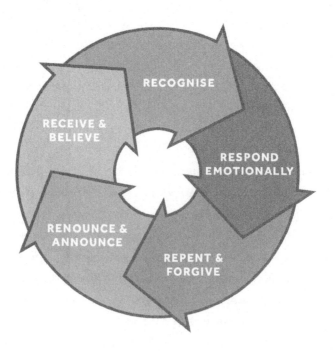

The Change Circle helps people respond when they recognise a moment of formation, a *discipleship moment*. It consists of five movements or actions that help us move towards Jesus and grow in Christlikeness.

Recognise

We've hit a discipleship moment. Maybe we've done something outwardly sinful. Perhaps we've been dishonest in order to manipulate someone, or verbally abused someone we were angry with. Or maybe it's a hidden, inward sin that no one else can see but that we're aware of in our own heart. Perhaps we've lusted over someone or pridefully judged a stranger or been gluttonous at a dinner party. Whatever has happened, conviction has set in, and we're wondering what to do next.

Many people are too busy or overwhelmed with life's responsibilities to stop at such moments and so quickly move on with a quick, whispered *"I'm sorry"* prayer to God to ease their conscience. Others may feel guilty and so avoid taking the time to process it with God. To truly change, however, we need to pay attention. It is a moment to put aside our busyness, push past the discomfort of feeling guilty, and go a bit deeper into the roots of the sin so that we're not just cheapening God's grace and failing to truly repent.

Paying attention gives room to ask questions like, *"How does God feel about this?" "Why have I acted like this?" "What does my response to this situation reveal about my beliefs?" "What lies have I believed about God, myself or others?" "What compels me to sin like this?"* It allows us to recognise ungodly patterns in our life or wrong thinking about God and who we are in Christ. It gives us space to ask the Holy Spirit if there is any part of the gospel we are not living in the light of, or are failing to embrace. I can't emphasise enough how important it is to get to the heart of the issue, not just the presenting sin.

Respond Emotionally

Secondly, we give ourselves permission to express our emotions. This involves asking, *"How do I feel right now?"* It's surprising how many of us struggle at this point. Perhaps we easily dismiss our feelings as untrustworthy or irrelevant. Maybe we've always chosen not to display emotional responses as this feels too vulnerable. Instead, we need to try to learn to identify and express our emotions and share with God how we feel about our behaviour or attitude. Maybe those sinful actions were in response to being hurt by people or feeling disappointment towards God or others. All these emotions need processing with God.

The Psalms are often so helpful at this point, giving us trustworthy grooves or tracks to run down when we don't know what to say. They provide safety and boundaries to the expression of our feelings. They allow us to acknowledge how important it is to express pain, anger, shame, disappointment, ungodly motives, grief, and hurt.[1]

We don't have to pretend it's okay when it isn't: God can cope with our feelings. In fact, God made us with emotional capacity and emotions are a gift. Over time, we can learn to be emotionally connected and to express our feelings healthily.

Repent and Forgive

The third stage is to ask God to show us anything we need to repent of and anybody we need to forgive. Repentance is a change of mind that leads to a change of heart and life. As we saw in Chapter 3, it involves turning from sin and moving towards God's best for our lives. Repentance is a joy because it's moving from my way to God's way.

Jesus links the way God treats us to the attitudes we should have towards others. *'Do not judge, and you will not be judged. Do not condemn, and you will not be condemned. Forgive, and you will be forgiven.'* (Luke 6:37) Just as

God forgives us our sins, we, too, need to forgive others and sometimes forgive ourselves.

Many years ago, I was discipling a friend who had been hurt by his previous church leader. The man had spent many hours with his pastor and believed a strong friendship had blossomed between them. He had confided deeply in the pastor, and their young families had spent lots of time together. While my friend didn't work for the church, he volunteered many hours a week. Trust was high and the two men had even led church services together. Then out of the blue, he discovered that the pastor had decided to leave the church for another leadership position. He had said nothing about it to my friend, who was left high and dry. The pastor's leaving was sudden and swift, and though there had been no actual abuse or manipulation, the deep hurt to my friend was caused by wrong expectations. He'd thought he was the pastor's friend, whereas the pastor saw the relationship as merely practical and functional.

Pinpointing who is at fault in a situation like this is tricky, as we all have different unspoken expectations in our relationships. However, as I listened to my friend's story, I could see the pain this episode had caused him, and the ongoing impact on his ability to trust people, particularly church leaders. He backed out of any church leadership responsibilities, and his bitterness towards his former pastor festered in his heart.

As we spent time talking this through and processing his feelings, we both realised he needed to choose to forgive the pastor. He might never really understand why the pastor had treated him like this, and he recognized that restoration was unlikely. Instead, my friend needed to stop going over and over those difficult moments in his mind, stop picking at the scab of disappointment and start the process of declaring his old pastor forgiven.

We led him in an initial prayer time as he brought the painful moments in that relationship before God. He forced himself to speak out his forgiveness as the internal battle raged inside. What was difficult was that he felt he was letting his pastor off the hook – it seemed so unfair to simply forgive him without making his pastor see how hurtful he had been. Yet, out of obedience to Jesus, he forgave him, and then chose to repeat this prayer over the coming weeks. Over time, I could see a lightness growing in my friend's life as his bitterness started to soften and he became more willing to trust others again.

Forgiveness costs, because when there is a loss, someone has to pay. This is the reason God does not simply "forgive and forget" our sin – there is a price to be paid. But the glorious message of the Gospel is that Jesus took our place and paid the price for our sin on the cross, so that we're no longer held liable for all that we've done wrong. In the same way, when someone wrongs us, we can either make *them* pay or decide to bear the cost *ourselves* and forgive the debt they owe us, just as God in Christ forgives the debt we owe him. When we choose to forgive someone, *we* bear the cost and agree no longer to hold them liable for the debt they owe us.

Forgiveness carries with it a sense of vulnerability, as we cannot control the other person's decisions or attitudes. They may never repent or apologise; they may go on making the same decisions to hurt or offend us. However, forgiveness is something we can choose to do; it is not contingent on the other person feeling sorry or changing their behaviour.

There is a saying, *"Unforgiveness is like drinking poison and waiting for your enemy to die"*. Jesus gives us the power to forgive and ultimately, forgiveness can set us free if we trust Jesus and make a choice. Not forgiving keeps you in a spiritual prison and ultimately hurts you. Instead, forgiveness is a choice; it is a process of identifying, cancelling the debt, and then releasing it.

On a human level, we might think that forgiving someone like this would leave us lacking. But the glorious upside-down kingdom of God, means that when we choose to forgive, yes, there will be an initial cost, but it will lead to a much greater blessing. There is great strength in being the first to forgive which, in God's kingdom, is ultimately for our benefit!

When we consider the areas in which we need to forgive someone, we should aim to be specific. And we should also be ready to acknowledge sin or wrong expectations of our own that may have contributed to the issue. In time, we will find that something shifts in us and, eventually, we can be free from the negative influence of those who sinned against us. In fact, I can tell when I've truly forgiven someone, because I no longer want to withhold good things from their life. I can bless them and no longer want bad things to happen to them.

Renounce and Announce

Tim Chester helpfully observes, '*Behind every sin is a lie about God and the gospel.*'[2] He's leaning into Romans 1, where the Apostle Paul suggests that sinful behaviour flows from exchanging the truth of God for a lie and worshipping created things rather than the Creator. Adam and Eve sinned in the garden because they believed a lie about the goodness of God: Satan told them, "*You shall not surely die,*" and they believed him (Genesis 3:4).

Our surface sin - the wrong we do, say and think on a daily basis - is not random: it's connected to a lie about the character and nature of God. It comes from not trusting (and enjoying) God and his Word. These lies may have come from things people have spoken over us or said to us, or they might come from challenging experiences we've been through.

Consciously or unconsciously, these lies about God get into our minds. They can feel solid and immovable; but ultimately, they have no real power. God's truth demolishes any argument or pretension that sets itself up against God.[3] Tim Chester summarises the four key truths to battle lies with:

God is Great–so we don't have to be in control.

God is Glorious–so we don't have to fear others.

God is Good–so we don't have to look elsewhere.

God Is Gracious–so we don't have to prove ourselves.[4]

Over and over again, I've seen people's lifelong lies wither when held up against the truth of God's word. Biblical truth is kryptonite to our untruths, so we must treasure it, memorise it, and actively put our trust in it.

This stage of the change circle is the moment to expose the lies we're believing and declare biblical truth. It is such a simple exercise but incredibly powerful. It often reveals how crazy we were to believe the lies in the first place. Renouncing lies breaks the shame that can attach itself to them. This part of the change circle is helping people take every thought captive as we examine every thought and hold it up against the light of the gospel and the character of God and decide whether we will allow that thought into our minds or not.[5]

Receive and believe:

We can invite the Holy Spirit to heal, fill, transform, and bring freedom. This is the moment to allow God to reveal his goodness and love. It opens the door to liberty and freedom where God can lavish us with grace, forgiveness and the power to live differently. We saw in Chapter 4 the power of encountering God. The Holy Spirit helps us to believe who we are in Christ and then live in light of this.

Nasty Neighbours

Imagine we're back in my old house, and I'm struggling with my neighbours. How does the change circle help me cooperate with God's agenda for my healing and growth?

Firstly I recognise the significance of this experience. Given there is no escape or quick way out (I can't move house overnight), it's essential to not look for quick fixes but to brace myself for a long journey of discipleship. This helps me to have realistic expectations and a willingness to lean into God long-term.

Secondly, I acknowledge the various emotions I feel at this moment. I bring them to God and try to find some friends to share them with. I journal, pray and sit in silence. I attempt to be brutally honest and specifically try to focus on how I feel about the situation, God and my actions. Sometimes I feel emotions deeply; other times, I feel nothing but either way, I try to express them in prayer or journalling.

Next, I repeatedly choose to repent from sinful thinking about the neighbours and decide to forgive them for their attitude and actions towards us. Some days this is easy (usually when things have been quiet for a while), and other days almost impossible. I try to confess my anger to God and try not to daydream about revenge or getting justice.

Fourth, it's crucial to renounce any lies I believe about God or the gospel. It's easy for me to feel unfairly treated by God or let down that he let us buy this house. These thoughts reveal the lies I'm choosing to believe about God's apparent lack of goodness. When I'm angry at God for letting this happen to us, I confess my wrong thinking about God and about my imagined immunity to suffering.

Instead, I announce the truth about my life with God. I focus on the idea that my reliance on God is forged in the crucible of trials and tests.[6] This is helpful language when the struggle is real. A crucible is a container in which metals are melted and subjected to very high temperatures. This process allows impurities (called the dross) to rise to the surface, so they can be skimmed off the top. What remains is purified and can be fashioned and modelled into its new shape and purpose. God uses suffering to purge away the dross in our lives and leads to our growth. I ask the Holy Spirit what he wants to reveal and transform in my life. I meditate on God's love for me when I was his enemy and ask if I could do the same.[7]

Lastly, I ask friends to pray for me to be filled with the Holy Spirit. I spend time in worship and rejoice in God's grace and goodness to me. I acknowledge my inability to survive this in my own strength and try to ask God to grow patience and love for my enemies.

Try this at home

Each time you experience a *'discipleship moment'*, you can use this change circle to guide you through the process. Even better, find a trusted friend to pray with you. Each time you complete the circle, you are aligning your life with Jesus and stepping into his transformation of your life. Increasingly you are becoming the person Jesus wants you to be.

For a free PDF of 'The Change Circle' visit www.matthatch.org

Questions

1. Can you identify a current situation in your life where you could practise using the Change Circle?

2. How do you normally process your emotions? How easy or difficult do you find it to express how you really feel towards God?

3. Is there anyone you know you need to forgive? How could you move towards making choices to forgive them?

---

1. Psalm 6:3-6; 10:1-2; 13:1-2; 44:23-26; 94:1-7

2. Tim Chester, 'You Can Change -God's transforming power for our sinful behaviour and negative emotions.' (IVP, 2008)

3. 2 Corinthians 10:3-5

4. Tim Chester, 'You Can Change -God's transforming power for our sinful behaviour and negative emotions.' - (IVP, 2008) p.87

5. 2 Corinthians 10:5

6. Proverbs 17:3

7. James 4:4

For more discipleship resources visit
www.matthatch.org

PART 3

How God changes us

SEQUOIA TREE BOOKS

"Many of us try to shove spiritual transformation into the nooks and crannies of a life that is already unmanageable, rather than being willing to arrange our life for what our heart most wants. We think that somehow we will fall into transformation by accident."

Ruth Haley Barton
(Sacred Rhythms: Arranging Our Lives for
Spiritual Transformation)

TEN

SPIRITUAL PATTERNS AND DISCIPLINES

In the early days of embracing discipleship, I began to learn what discipleship guru Dallas Willard describes as '*the secret of the easy yoke*.'[1] Dallas had observed how often Christians would read about the Sermon on the Mount[2] and then try just to live it without engaging in any training or spiritual preparation. They would try not to worry or lust or get angry with people in the moment. They'd aim to love their neighbours as themselves and give to the needy; while at the same time live exactly the same as the non-Christians around them. They'd literally have no thought of intentionally training in the *way* of Jesus to equip them to do the *works* of Jesus. They'd miss the invitation to take up the easy yoke of life with Christ.

It makes total sense - if we are expected to do the stuff that Jesus did (make disciples, heal the sick, stand up against religious corruption, love the poor, witness to others) but we don't adopt Jesus' lifestyle and example, then we're never going to be radical disciples. All this meant I needed to think holistically about my life and embrace Jesus' way of doing life if I wanted to do what Jesus did. By accident, I'd stumbled on the main way that God changes us.

Three important ingredients

I've never been an athlete or talented sportsman. However, I once was picked to represent my primary school at the age of eleven in our local *'who can throw a cricket ball the furthest'* competition (I didn't win). The little I do know about training for any physical activity or sport is that it takes a combination of something to motivate you (I want to lose some weight, I want to be able to run 5k), some intention (this is bigger than simply wanting to do it, intention means you actually *do* something), and finally, some habits or activities to engage in (you can't sit there and do nothing, you need to start running).

These three things, *vision, intention and activity,* are essential not just to improve in sports but also to see transformation in our lives. For Christians, our *vision* is to be with Jesus. Our *intention* is the Spirit-inspired inner motivation to become more Christlike, and the *activities* or methods of transformation are what we are historically called the spiritual disciplines.[3]

Vision

I think the majority of us skip the *vision* part of this process, but if we do, we can easily become overwhelmed and discouraged by the effort required to engage with spiritual formation because we lose sight of the finish line. Let me remind us that I believe the most satisfying, life-giving, peace-filled life I could live is found in a relationship with Jesus. This is the ultimate Christian vision.

Yet, I also find another vision of life on earth distracting me. One where I live *independently* of Jesus. On my terms. For my comfort. For my enjoyment - which means I seek life, satisfaction and joy in all the wrong places instead of being with him. Even my *'spiritual life'* can lead me away from God and into doing stuff for legalistic reasons, to bolster my own sense of worth, out of fear of others, or through living with guilt, rather than because of Jesus.

To counteract this, I need to keep reminding myself of how good the gospel invitation is. In the words of writers Don Simpson and Dallas Willard, *Jesus invites us to leave our burdensome ways of heavy labour - especially our religious ones - and step into the yoke of training with him. His is a way of gentleness and lowliness, a way of soul rest. His is a way of inner transformation in which carrying our burden with him is easy and light. What we thought was so difficult about entering fully into the divine life is entirely due to our failure to understand and take the small steps that quietly but surely lead to our transformation...no one needs to live in spiritual and personal defeat. A life of victory over sin and circumstance is accessible to us all.*[4]

This invitation is both beautiful and empowering when we truly embrace it. Our attitude to this vision of life with Jesus will reveal our hearts. If that reminder, of how good the 'good news' of the gospel is, doesn't sound that fulfilling, then it suggests that other things have captured our hearts. Our desires have been hijacked and we will find the work to become more Christlike lifeless and unsustainable. Yet if the vision is clear and trusted, we'll be motivated to pursue and discover the disciplines for ourselves.

Intention

To intend to do something means to do what's needed to do it. We may have thought about doing lots of things but never intended to do them, so they remain undone. There's a whole lot of difference between thinking or planning on dieting and *actually* dieting. The difference is intention.

For transformation to happen, we need to ask the Holy Spirit to empower and motivate us to move from thinking about changing to engaging in the change process.

Desire

Have you ever had the experience of learning something new at church that inspires you to live differently, but within a day or so, you're back in the same patterns and behaviours? It's because information or knowledge alone doesn't change us. There is a big disconnect between what we *know* and what we *do*. What we do is shaped more by what we want or desire.

Sociologist James KA Smith says that humans are primarily desiring beings. We're *'first and foremost lovers.'* [5] It means the things we love, desire and want are the things that motivate us at a deep level. We move in the direction of our primary desires, which are usually for life to be good and for us to be happy and content. It's a desire that could ultimately lead us to God, but there are many competing claims in the world.

Smith also says we are intentional beings and aim our lives at a vision shaped by our desires. In other words, our desires and intentions point us in a specific direction.

Crucially, our primal drive is influenced by the habits in our lives and the things we are constantly engaged in and surrounded by (Smith calls them *'cultural liturgies'*).

You notice it as you walk around a shopping mall and immerse yourself in a world selling you a lifestyle full of luxury gadgets, smells, and clothes. You begin wanting things you never set out to desire. This is why advertising is so powerful. Smith argues that these patterns, liturgies, and disciplines are shaping us, aiming us in a specific direction and influencing our decisions. They are, in effect, discipling us.

Sadly, many of us are driven by what we want rather than what we believe. These misdirected loves lead to misdirected lives. We end up satisfied with created things rather than with our Creator. In discipleship, we must help shape our God-given desire so that we normally and naturally want what God desires.

Patterns, relationships, activities and disciplines

To this end, we have patterns, relationships, activities, and disciplines that point us towards God's kingdom. They shape our desires. We find a list of such activities in Acts 2:42: *'They devoted themselves to the apostles' teaching (a practice) and to fellowship (relationships), to the breaking of bread (experience) and to prayer (practice).'*

These activities, or *spiritual disciplines*, help us follow Jesus intentionally when we arrange our whole lives around them in a similar way to Jesus. Jesus prayed, so we pray. Jesus memorised scripture, so we memorise scripture. Jesus fasted, so we fast, and so forth. He embraced these patterns, relationships, activities and disciplines to grow in maturity.

At their best, spiritual disciplines connect us with God's grace, which changes us. At their worst, we can end up obsessing over how much or how little we have engaged in them and forget that the whole point is to help us be with Jesus and love others as we love ourselves. The power isn't in the practice. Spiritual disciplines are a gateway to Jesus and the abundant life he offers us. As writer Matt Smethurst writes, '*They don't make you more treasured by God. They're about making God more treasured by you.*'[6] Spiritual disciplines are how we cooperate with God in the sanctification process. It's important to remember that effort (our actions) is not the same thing as earning (our attitude).

I understand that for some people this can sound difficult and unpleasant, but we're simply aligning ourselves with the things we truly want. For example, I want to love my wife and enjoy our relationship. Therefore, we practise certain activities and patterns to help us flourish. We have regular catch-ups, plan our diaries, eat meals together, apologise when we hurt each other and take holidays every now and then. Some of these things are very mundane but they contribute to a happier, deeper marriage. Spiritual disciplines function in the same way towards God. They position us to be *with* him.

And if you're still not convinced, let me be blunt. We all face a certain pain in this life. There is no avoiding it. We can choose the pain of discipline or the pain of regret. We can either embrace activities that train us in godliness or we can sit back, do nothing, and live with the pain of a wasted, untransformed life. It obviously feels much easier to put off that decision to pray or fast or turn off the TV, but that short-term satisfaction will eventually be overcome by long-term spiritual stagnation. My hope is that we will choose to pursue what we've been made for rather than what we want right now.

A Rule of Life

This combination of vision, intention and activity leads to the formation of what the ancient writers called *a rule of life*. This is simply a commitment to crafting our life so that we live it in the way God has called us to. It's practically applying what it means to be with Jesus, become like Jesus and then live like Jesus.

The word *'rule'* can be off-putting, but behind it is the idea of a trellis. Plants, especially vines, need a trellis to guide their growth and help them to flourish. A *'trellis of life'* makes a bit more sense when we think about what is needed to help us cooperate fully with God and live wholeheartedly for him. We will look in chapters 10, 11 and 12 at the sort of rhythms and relationships that help us develop a rule of life.

Training to be like Jesus

You've probably discovered that we cannot expect, in the moment, to behave like Christ. We cannot simply adjust an internal dial or control our actions, thoughts, or feelings. To try and change our heart response *in* the moment is impossible. Instead, we must *train* by adopting Jesus' training methods.

The disciplines help develop a spiritual 'muscle memory'. In fact, all formation requires repetition. What we repeatedly do has the greatest formative power to shape our lives. It's hidden and subtle, but practice makes perfect. Most of us don't think about how to pick up a pen, smile, or type a text: we do it by muscle memory because we've done it thousands of times. Using these spiritual disciplines is similarly meant to help us naturally and normally react to situations in a godly way because we've done the hard work of training before the event actually happens.

For example, when I'm cycling to work, and someone cuts me up in their car or nearly runs me over, I want to shout at them or (more honestly) pull them out of their car and shake some sense into them. If I've not trained myself in godliness, that sort of response is more likely to happen.

But if I've spent time memorising, *"You have heard that it was said, 'Love your neighbour and hate your enemy.' But I tell you, love your enemies and pray for those who persecute you, that you may be children of your Father in heaven.'"* (Matthew 5:43-44); if I repeatedly forgive other careless drivers (my 'enemies'); if I remind myself that I'm not always faultless in the way I cycle; and if I ask for the Holy Spirit to fill me with peace and love: over time, if I do these things every day, I develop the habit of responding well. So when the moment comes, and a car cuts me up, maybe my spiritual muscle memory will mean I'll respond with grace. In this sense, I'm genuinely a practising Christian. I'm practising all the time to be like Jesus.

If this is true, it means we can celebrate every part of our transformation rather than just waiting till the end when we eventually become more Christlike. Training (rather than trying) celebrates every time we choose to do the right thing. For example, we may want to grow in purity. There will hopefully be a day when we don't look at people and lust after them. But when we're training, each time we choose not to click on that alluring clickbait on the internet, and each time we turn our mind away from lust is a win. If we're training, each obedient choice means we're doing better than before. Sure, we're not the finished article, but as we simply turn up and work on our transformation, God is cheering us on!

The *'training not trying'* principle is so vital for Christians to embrace. Grace means we're saved without having to do anything to earn or deserve it, but we must still practise and train ourselves for godliness. Too many Christians assume their spiritual growth works in the same way as salvation, that we just do nothing and expect God to transform us. In effect, we have made grace into something that paralyses us, rather than something that should spur us to change our lives. In fact, our character is mainly changed over time through patterns, relationships, activities, and disciplines that point us towards God's kingdom.

What makes something a discipline?

I've often used this definition of discipline that originates from Dallas Willard. *"It is an activity in my power, which enables me to accomplish what I cannot do by direct effort."*[7]

Let me explain. When my kids were younger, they knew we kept the biscuits in a tin on top of the kitchen cupboards. However hard they tried to reach the tin on their own, standing on tiptoes, it was out of reach. But simply by dragging a stool over to the kitchen worktop, they could climb the stool, stand on it, and reach the biscuits. The *stool* is like the discipline or activity. It helped them do what they couldn't do by willpower or trying really hard. All spiritual disciplines work in this way.

It is impossible to simply jump from being a prideful person to one that is humble, or from a greedy person to a generous one. But there are small things in our power that, if practised regularly over time, can move us towards a more Christlike life. These patterns, activities, relationships or disciplines expose us to the grace and power of the Holy Spirit, and it is this that changes us internally. The spiritual disciplines are an intentional, focused way of standing under the waterfall of grace, love and power that flows from heaven's throne.

I love to imagine it that way. Every time I read my Bible, worship God, or fast and pray, these are worthy things to do in and of themselves, but at the same time, I'm being led by that activity into the love and grace of God that transforms me. This is why historically, the disciplines have been known as a *'means of grace'*. They simply move us into the presence of God. Over time, as we encounter God, we find him changing our desires and perspective. We begin to love the things he loves and do what he wants us to do. We start to shed disobedience and habitual sin.

It's these repeated patterns, relationships, activities, and disciplines that will make us into a different sort of person. If we want to experience transformation, we must change up our patterns and repeat as needed. If we want to be formed into greater Christlikeness, we need to adopt some new activities that train us that way. It's a bit like learning to drive a car. At first, every action seems clunky and confusing until, with practice, it starts to become second nature, and we no longer have to think consciously about which pedal to press, or how to signal and turn right. Godliness can feel equally difficult at first, but with time, practice, and effort, there will be areas of life where we naturally and normally act in a godly way without thinking about it.

Effort is required

I think the spiritual disciplines are somewhat self-authenticating. Once we embrace them for a season, there is no turning back. Over time we see their impact and potential to bring lasting change.

The problem is that we can think of the effort required in growth as 'anti-gospel' or 'anti-grace'. Or we may have a faith where God is invited into our hearts in a limited way, and therefore any energetic and intentional training for godliness seems unnecessary or over the top. We think that is just for keen people. Or we may need to detox from our Western, consumer-driven culture that tells us the church exists to serve us and make Christianity as comfortable and doable as possible. At Mosaic, we regularly give examples of how people invest in the disciplines at different stages of life in a way that derives from a foundation of grace.

Descent and Ascent.

Transformational discipleship also involves a descent and an ascent. Jesus made clear there was a descent, a dying and emptying that leads to life. The New Testament describes this descent as *'the mortification of the flesh.*[8] The word *'mortify'* means *'to put to death by degrees'*. It's related to the word *'mortgage'*. When we pay off our mortgage each month, we put the debt to death bit by bit. In the same way, if we follow Jesus, we are putting to death our old sinful self one step at a time (descending) to gain our true resurrection life (ascending). The spiritual disciplines help us with this movement. We practise activities such as fasting, simplicity, solitude and silence that help us die to our agendas and preferences in order to gain Christ's.

The disciplines that help us with the other half of the process, the ascent, include Bible memorisation, worship, and generosity. These lead to a filling and growing in our spiritual life and position us before God who brings strength, endurance, joy and freedom.

Disclaimer

Even though I wholeheartedly agree with the above, I also want us to understand that we cannot simply plan, control or manage our spiritual formation ourselves. If we approach these disciplines simply to engineer an outcome, we're succumbing to 'project self' - the idea that if we do this and that, then hey presto, we're Christlike.

As we all know, we can't 'microwave' godliness. We can't click a button and have holiness delivered to our door within hours. Spiritual formation takes desire, intention, and spiritual activities, plus lots (and lots) of time. I've learnt recently that great English oak trees spend three hundred years growing, three hundred years resting, and three hundred years gracefully dying. Organic growth is slow. Spiritual growth too, just takes time.

Wouldn't it be great if the way to spiritual growth was as simple as attending a conference, hearing a fantastic talk, or receiving the Spirit in a powerful ministry moment? I love all the above, but I've often come home from them and found within minutes that my sinful habits haven't changed. My passion fades and my zeal is lost.

Instead, we need to remember that spiritual growth is seasonal and slow. It also takes skill to determine what disciplines are needed at what times. If I were trying to grow my biceps, it would be of little value to be concentrating on squats or sit-ups. In the same way, the thing we're training in (becoming less prideful, greedy, lustful, or impatient) should determine the disciplines we engage in. This means we don't just randomly pick up a discipline and engage in it; rather, we pick the activity that will specifically train us in that area.

It takes between twenty and eighty days to form a new habit, so we need to be patient. That's half a month to three months of practice before we start to do the new thing naturally and normally. We need to be gentle with ourselves and just keep plodding. Additionally, we should take note of the season, age and stage of life we find ourselves in. What we can pull off as a single student will vary hugely from what we can manage as a parent with young children, low on energy and capacity.

In one sense, we start at where we want to be and use the disciplines (things in our power) to move us towards where God intends us to be. For example, the opposite to a prideful person is a humble person. Sadly it's impossible to become humble overnight (I've tried). But certain disciplines will particularly help us grow in humility, for example: serving others in secret; memorising Philippians 2:3-11; confessing prideful thoughts to a trusted friend; investing in someone else; letting others go first and get the applause. All these will move us towards being the humble person God wants us to be. It is specific and focused, designed to train you in godliness. This principle can be applied to all areas where we need to see transformation. We need to choose the disciplines that will change our heart.

Many of the ancient spiritual writers also recommended choosing a particular area in which we are seeking growth or freedom, and to concentrate on that for an extended period, rather than trying to change various areas all at once. So a person might focus on truthfulness, gentleness, or humility, identifying the key practices that will help them in that regard, and focusing on that for an appropriate length of time.

What the disciplines aren't.

To summarise, spiritual disciplines are not a way to earn favour with God, or to earn brownie points in heaven. But they are wonderful pathways to experience God's life-changing love.

The disciplines are not necessarily unpleasant. What makes something a discipline depends on what we are training for. We can get into thinking that for a discipline to count, it must be something we don't want to do, and that it usually involves pain; however, this is simply not the case. Many of us would probably benefit from taking a proper, regular sabbath or celebrating the goodness of God with our favourite worship song or psalm.

The disciplines are not necessarily a barometer of spirituality. Many people think that God measures their spiritual performance by how well they perform certain disciplines. Think of a basketball player who doesn't get any points for the number of shots that go in during practice. The only reason to practise is to shoot better in the game. It's the same for us to some degree. Practising disciplines should help us love God and others better, which is what really counts.

Questions:

1. Can you identify one area of your life where you need to grow in godliness, or have previously struggled to experience transformation? What activities could you stop or start doing to train yourself in this area?

2. Do you have a clear vision for growth and transformation? To help you clarify it, you might find it helpful to write it out or explain it to someone else.

3. What has been your experience of spiritual disciplines up to now? Have you been encouraged by engaging with any of them? If so, how could this motivate your next steps?

4. Or have you had negative experiences of trying spiritual disciplines? If so, given what you know now, can you identify what went wrong and why? How could you move past this discouragement and engage more positively with spiritual disciplines from here on?

5. What do you think of the idea of developing a "rule of life"? What patterns, relationships, activities and disciplines could help you in this?

6. Could you try and take some time out in the next few days, to quietly reflect on what the Holy Spirit is saying to you?

---

1. Dallas Willard, The Divine Conspiracy - Rediscovering our hidden life with God' (Harper One, 2009)

2. Matthew 5-7

3. This idea originally comes from Dallas Willard, who describes the Spiritual disciplines as consisting of Vision, Intention and Method.

4. Don Simpson & Dallas Willard 'Revolution of Character' (Navigators Press, 2014), p.11

5. James K Smith, 'You are what you love: The Spiritual power of habits' (Grand Rapids, MI: Brazos, 2016) p.2

6. Matt Smethurst Tweet 2:45 pm · 7 Sep 2021

7. Dallas Willard, Renewing the Christian Mind: Essays, Interviews, and Talks (New York, NY: HarperCollins Publishers, 2016), p.283.

8. Romans 8:13; Colossians 3:5

"There is no friend closer than Jesus.
As we follow him, he never strides too
far ahead. He never dodges or ditches
us. If we are weary, he slows. If we pull
up lame, he stops. If we wander, he
circles back. He won't let us be lost."

Jared C Wilson
(Friendship with the Friend
of Sinners)

ELEVEN

(UP) RELATIONSHIP WITH GOD

I have two trees in my garden that couldn't be more different. Our little sycamore grew all by itself. A whirling seed pod must have landed in a plant plot and it slowly came to life. It has grown on its own, and you can tell. The main trunk is twisted and curved. It has decided to grow in one direction and then changed its mind and developed in another. It's bent and leaning slightly because of the wind. I'm not sure if it's going to survive long term.

Our other tree, a hornbeam, was planted intentionally. Hornbeams are beautiful trees whose branches fan out in a perfect heart shape. It has two strong stakes in the ground on either side of it. The main trunk is attached with an adjustable strap and it has rubber buffers to stop it from scraping against the support. It is straight and strong. We're fully confident it will outlast us.

I think you know where I'm going with this. The stakes supporting the hornbeam are like the rhythms, activities and disciplines in our lives. They help us grow in the right direction. When used correctly, they lead to flourishing and fruit. Without them, our growth is haphazard, influenced by the latest spiritual wind, and may not last the test of time.

The following three chapters look at the tools of discipleship we have at our disposal. These tools or disciplines describe how we fight for spiritual formation. At Mosaic, we often talk about the UP, IN and OUT of the Christian life.

They are a quick way of referring to the worship, community and mission that every church is called to engage in. I've separated these biblical tools into these categories.

The tools we use in the UP are directed towards God. They are focused on our worship and relationship with the Trinity.

The IN focuses on the tools we use together in the Christian community as we love each other.

The OUT is directed towards the world and the people we're called to love and serve.

Please note, however, that in one sense, most of the tools and disciplines should be practised with others. Also, this is not an exhaustive list; rather, they are the essential tools we have found to be most helpful in experiencing lasting transformation.

Here are a few essential (UP) activities that can form the supporting trellis for a life of growth.

1) Personal Devotions

Many years ago, I met a famous pastor whose ministry I had admired from afar. I had bought his books, listened to many of his sermons and was impressed by the number of people reached through his church. I was so nervous when we finally met that I managed to say hello using my name (instead of his) and introduce myself using his name. I don't know if you've ever made that mistake, but the most typical reaction would be for both of us to laugh. Instead, I quickly realised that he wasn't even listening. His lack of warmth and eye contact, as we shook hands, told me this man didn't care and wasn't interested in me at all. It was a very awkward few seconds as the guy brushed me off and moved on.

Now, I wasn't expecting to be greeted as if we were long-lost friends. Nor did I want him to spend hours with me, giving me some personal advice and pastoral wisdom. I guess I was simply expecting a tiny level of engagement that communicated a hint of friendliness. Looking back, maybe he was having a bad day, or was 'peopled out', or feeling unwell. I hope it wasn't something he regularly did. What did happen is that my affection for him and his work, and my desire to get time with him, faded in an instant.

God is not like this man. When we spend time with God, we are never met with a harsh, withdrawn, uncommunicative God. He isn't fickle or 'peopled out'. He won't disappoint or quickly move on. In fact, it's quite the opposite. He desires to be with us. He's not just friendly when we show up, he's longing for us to be present with him. He wants a relationship with us, his beloved. His door is always open. The unchanging God who made the universe beckons us into deep, intimate communion.

Quality time

Jesus models a life of intimacy with God. *'Very early in the morning, while it was still dark, Jesus got up, left the house and went off to a solitary place, where he prayed.'* (Mark 1:35) The gospel writer, Luke, wants his readers to know the source of Jesus' power - *'Yet the news about him spread all the more, so that crowds of people came to hear him and to be healed of their sicknesses. But Jesus often withdrew to lonely places and prayed.'* (Luke 5:15-16)

There are even a few times where we hear Jesus' prayers out loud; before his arrest and a little later when he sweated blood and wrestled with submitting to his Father's will.[1] In busyness, stress, preparation and normality, Jesus prioritised time with God daily. He spent all his time with God *and* had unique, quality time with God.

His desire was for his disciples to follow his way of life. He even tells them, *'Remain in me, as I also remain in you. No branch can bear fruit by itself; it must remain in the vine. Neither can you bear fruit unless you remain in me.'* (John 15:4). His disciples are to remain attached, connected, and grow from a place of dependence on God. Just like Jesus, we are to seek quality time with God to deepen our relationship. This is what I mean by a devotional time.

Yet we often struggle with this aspect of following Jesus. Many of us have struggled to respond habitually to God's invitation to be with him. A 2014 survey of Evangelical Christians in the UK revealed that over 50% of those surveyed only spent six to nine minutes daily with God praying.[2]

Our experiences of devotional times are often laden with failure, guilt and pressure. Some of us feel that planned or scheduled time with God feels fake and unreal. When encouraged to push through negative feelings, others say their time with God feels forced and legalistic. Some of us have no motivation or expectation for these times because we are so weary or busy. Or our season of life (parenting, caring for others, exams) means we've got no time or have other priorities. I've spoken with people with high expectations that were never realised, so they're disappointed. My anecdotal studies from Mosaic are that many of us feel like failures in this department - we've tried and failed repeatedly.

Enjoyable and doable

So how do we practise these disciplines of grace and help others do the same? I've found the key to a healthy devotional life is finding the best time of day when we are most free from everything else. Pick a regular spot if possible. Make it as enjoyable and doable as possible. My secret is the same seat, warm blanket, hot tea in my favourite mug, and dark chocolate. It all helps get me out from under my duvet and before my Maker. I try to go to bed earlier to get enough sleep and feel fresher in the morning.

Of course, this is the ideal scenario, and some days are a write-off. The idea, though, is to create space for this time with God as often as possible, which creates momentum over the long haul.

Even if initially (being brutally honest) we don't *want* to be with God, regular devotional time will help *cultivate* a passion for Him. When a couple falls in love, there are hormonal fireworks. But when married, they must cultivate delight in one another. We can fall out of love with God through lack of investment, just as a husband or wife can fall out of love with their spouse.

There can be a weariness which, if left unaddressed, can lead to spiritual adultery, where we fall out of love with God and substitute him with something else. Often our devotional times feel mundane and average. We can feel like we're failing when heaven is silent and God is distant. But over time, the regular habit of being with God cements his place in our hearts. I encourage people to start with ten minutes every day. Once we've mastered that, we can increase it to fifteen. Over time, it will become a regular part of our day.

I remember a lady called Hannah who had always struggled to spend time with God consistently. She initially feared the commitment to something she associated with legalism. She needed to understand the heart of God towards her, so we spent time looking at one of the most breathtaking verses in the Old Testament. *'For the eyes of the Lord range throughout the earth to strengthen those whose hearts are fully committed to him.'* (2 Chronicles 16:9a). What an amazing truth - that God's eyes scan the earth looking for people who will seek him out. Hannah was moved to think beyond her hang-ups and see God's posture towards her. It was lifegiving and freeing for her to know the Father was patiently and lovingly waiting for her to lift her gaze towards him.

2) Meditating on God's Word

Once we get time with God, how does he communicate with us, and what should we spend our time doing? One activity is meditating on scripture. So rich is the transformative power of the Bible that Jesus prays to the Father, *'Sanctify them by the truth; your word is truth'* (John 17:17). Psalm 1 encourages us to delight and meditate in the law of the Lord. The psalmist likens the person who does this to a tree beside a stream that never withers and produces fruit at the right time. The Bible changes us, sustains us, and strengthens us. It is one of the main ways God speaks to us and reveals his will.

Jesus was sent into the wilderness to fast, pray and battle against the devil. His only sustenance was meditating on the book of Deuteronomy. Despite ravaging hunger, a sun-scorched desert and his ability to call on his Father to conjure up some food on demand, Jesus faithfully declares, *"It is written, 'Man shall not live by bread alone, but by every word that proceeds from the mouth of God."* (Matthew 4:4) Jesus believed God's word was more important than all other needs and wants.

At the heart of the Christian faith is a God who chooses to *reveal* himself to humankind. Chiefly this is through Jesus Christ, the Word of God. Jesus perfectly reflects God the Father to us. God also reveals himself through the written word. The Bible is unique, authoritative and personal. Our Bibles are *"...God-breathed and useful for teaching, rebuking, correcting, and training in righteousness, so that the servant of God may be thoroughly equipped for every good work"* (2 Timothy 3:16). The Holy Spirit used actual people, and all their experiences and personalities, to speak to us. The Bible is unique, authoritative and personal. Therefore, through spending time in scripture, we meet God and hear his voice.

However, even though we nod in agreement to the power of scripture to change us, we can often have a transactional rather than a formational relationship with the Bible. Like a bank account, we expect our investment of time and attention to the Word will reap an immediate sense of inspiration and the presence of God.[3] We want instant gratification. Sadly, thinking this way can lead to disillusionment and a crushing sense of guilt and failure. We grow weary quickly and lose heart. Or we persevere but only focus on simple passages with an immediate emotional or intellectual reward.

Instead, we must slow down and prepare to enjoy a more extended, tastier meal. Think seven-course dinner rather than a quick, cheap microwave meal. Donald Whitney, author of the modern classic 'Spiritual Disciplines for the Christian Life' said, *'No Spiritual Discipline is more important than the intake of God's Word. Nothing can substitute for it. There simply is no healthy Christian life apart from a diet of the milk and meat of Scripture.'*[4]

All forms of engagement in the Word are good, but I'd encourage you to learn how to meditate on scripture. Bible meditation isn't trying to empty our minds to attain a zen-like state. Rather it's slowly and deliberately lingering in God's word, maybe over a short passage, a single verse or even a word. I was always taught that cows have four stomachs to eke out every morsel of goodness from the grass they eat. Maybe this is a genius way to think about meditating on scripture. Slowly chewing over it and allowing the Spirit to reveal God to us.

I recently noticed that a friend had begun to pray, quoting various Bible passages. I found it a delight to intercede with him as his expectation and boldness had grown so much. He would use Bible passages to beseech God with phrases like *"You promise this in your Word, so Lord, we ask that you would do it now."* I found my faith growing when I was around him. His secret was that he had started to meditate on the Bible regularly. He would let small chunks of scripture infiltrate into his prayers. I rarely hear him pray now without quoting the Bible. It's not to show off or impress, it's because God's word has taken root in his mind and heart, and the overflow is powerful, contagious faith.

Where to start?

The scripture study model, the 'Discovery Bible Study' (DBS), is helpful when meditating on scripture or reading it with someone else. It helps us spend time in the Bible but avoids the pitfalls of simply hearing God's word and not applying it to our lives. It follows a simple model where we read any text and answer these four questions.

1. What does it tell us about God or Jesus?

2. What does it tell us about ourselves or people?

3. What am I going to do in response to reading this?

4. Who am I going to share this with?

We've found reading the verses a few times before answering the questions helps to focus on the passage. It often helps to write down our answers to the final two questions, especially if we want some accountability and feedback loops. This method helps move us from just hearing to doing.

3) Fasting and Prayer (with others)

Fasting is definitely out of fashion. I meet very few people who regularly fast for spiritual reasons. The reason isn't hard to find: we love eating and hate the pangs of hunger. We're surrounded by food; we can order it to our door within minutes. Eating is cathartic, comforting and necessary. Who doesn't want to indulge in their favourite foods? Why on earth would we repress our desire to eat good food?

Interestingly, while spiritual fasting is rare, health fasting is commonplace. I regularly bump into people doing intermittent fasting, Keto, or some sort of cleansing fast. Fasting is about getting healthier, purging your system, and losing weight. Fasting, or hunger striking, is also used as a means of protest. If someone is fasting in that way, it's usually their last resort to get the authorities or the media to pay attention to their cause.

For Christians, fasting is sometimes considered legalistic and unnecessary under the new covenant of grace. There are also multitudinous complications, as many of us have some sort of eating disorder or health issues. I have a complicated relationship with food and body image, and so it's easy to simply ignore the call to fast.

However, Jesus expects us to fast. In a challenging series of instructions in Matthew 6, Jesus covers an essential checklist for the Christian life and how he instructs us to live. He says, *'When you pray... when you forgive... when you give... when you seek first the kingdom... when you fast.'* Clearly, Jesus thought fasting was something as normative as giving and praying.

What's the point of fasting?

Fasting is going without food for a spiritual purpose. It is basically feasting on God. Fasting is going without food to increase our appetite for God. Food is a wonderful gift from God, but sometimes we need more of the giver than the gift. Of course, many of us apply fasting to other things we choose to forego. People will fast from social media for Lent - however, while beneficial, this isn't entirely the kind of fasting Jesus modelled and spoke about. He simply centred on food (or the lack of it). In scripture, we find examples of either a complete fast (no water or food), a normal fast (no food) or a partial fast (only simple foods).

My friend Daniel had always struggled with fasting. Naturally skinny, he found his weight dropped dramatically if he didn't eat. He was self-conscious and didn't want to lose the gains he'd made in the gym. It took some convincing for him to join our discipleship group in fasting together once a week. However, he immediately noticed a few things happening.

First, he realised for the first time that he needed to bring his body image issues to God. He wanted to repent where he'd put body image before obedience to God. Second, while finding the actual fasting day difficult, he noticed a growing spiritual authority, especially when praying for people. As he grew in faith for God to meet his needs in fasting, so he grew in faith for God to be at work in others. Lastly, he found self-control growing in other parts of his life. His devotional life grew more consistent and his willingness to obey the promptings of the Spirit increased.

Exposing what controls us

We fast to lean into God. It's a bit like putting on noise-cancelling headphones and turning the volume up to hear from God. I've done quite a few long fasts, and by day six, it's beautiful. You feel energised. I love the freedom and focus fasting brings.

Fasting switches off the autopilot and helps us see what is hidden when we are full. Richard Foster explains, *"More than any other single discipline, fasting reveals the things that control us."*[5] Fasting shows my addictions and the things I turn to for comfort. Many of us medicate our pain, hurt, and emotions with food. Food can be like an anaesthetic. When we have had a bad morning, we look forward to having a nice lunch to make us feel better. Going without food exposes our pain, pride, anger, relationship dissatisfaction, fear of failure, and emptiness. At first, we rationalise it, blaming the lack of food, but if we are honest, we know we are simply showing everyone our sinful selves. Sadly, when I fast, Philippa says it feels like she has to brace herself. She says that all my bad stuff comes out and impacts the family. I can't hide it. My impatience, stubbornness, and pride all come to the surface.

Yet while fasting, we can find freedom. Even though our appetites and desires can flow out of control, fasting brings balance and order. The Apostle Paul said, *'I will not be mastered by anything'* in 1 Corinthians 6:12. He even declares that he beats his body and makes it his slave in order for it to be under the lordship of Christ.[6] The power of fasting helps by *"dethroning king stomach"* and teaching us that we don't have to worship and obey our desires and wants.[7]

When we fast, we're focusing our desire back onto God. It connects us to our weaknesses. It reminds us we need to hunger for God: *'"My food," said Jesus, "is to do the will of him who sent me and to finish his work."'* (John 4:34) So many things in life take away our appetite for God and his purposes. Fasting is so powerful because it kills our cultural cravings. Food and culture can distract us from the real emptiness in the heart that can only be filled with God's presence. Fasting forces us to trust God.

Fundamentally, fasting is essential to training the will. Learning to say no to our hunger cravings strengthens our will overall, and enables us to more easily say no to our impulses more generally.

How prayer changes us

Prayer goes hand in hand with fasting. Prayer is where we commune with God and become more like him. Let's be honest, though - prayer can sometimes feel frustrating and even tedious. Our attention spans are so small that it can seem impossible to keep on a single line of thought without jumping off into random places in our minds. I can feel confused when my prayers are sometimes answered in the way I expected and others aren't. Fortunately, when we pray with God, there is a deeper purpose at work.

Prayer is transformational as God uses it to align our will to his. It humbles us. It helps us lay down our wants and desires and submit them to Jesus. Prayer is so difficult that it makes us come to God open-handed and ask for the Holy Spirit to teach and empower us to pray.

Prayer also makes us patient and helps us go at God's pace instead of ours. We often want God to answer our prayers in our way and in our timing. Discipleship expert Richard Foster explains: *'As we are learning to pray we discover an interesting progression. In the beginning our will is in struggle with God's will. We beg. We pout. We demand. We expect God to perform like a magician or shower us with blessings like Father Christmas. We major in instant solutions and manipulative prayers. In time, however, we begin to enter into a grace-filled releasing of our will and a flowing into the will of the Father.*[8] Prayer is a journey into consistently saying *'yes'* to God.

Prayer also makes us other-centred and generates compassion for others. When we pray for others, we lose some of our self-centeredness and start empathising with those around us. It is no surprise that the famous Clapham Sect, with their pursuit of social justice, the abolition of slavery and a deep compassion for others, spent three hours a day in prayer. Those of us who are activists and campaigners, who love to crack on and get things done, can easily forget the power of prayer and its ability to align our hearts to God's and move the mountains of injustice.

How to start praying and fasting?

To begin fasting, I've found starting gradually helps adjust to the challenges of going without food. Start with missing a meal and spending the time it would have taken to prepare and eat it in prayer. Move to fasting for a twenty-four-hour period once a week. Or even try a two-day fast at the start of every month. It may be good to tie in with the church's calendar in Lent and aim for a longer, more intentional fast.

Given the impact on the body, it is worth planning a fast so we're not too busy or preoccupied with other things. We may also want to speak to someone we trust to talk through our fast or even consult a doctor to check if our medical conditions comply with our fasting.

Try to pay attention to any wrong motives behind your fast. Very few people have perfect motives when it comes to going without food. I struggle with being motivated to lose weight. Bring these doubts, sinful attitudes or wrong motivations to God honestly. Talk to God about them and ask for his help to see the godly reasons for fasting and the correlation between your physical life and spiritual life.

As you fast, observe the attitude of your heart. Often food masks our impatience or lack of contentment. Think about what God is revealing to you and what needs to change. Above all, try to keep going, even when experiencing hunger pains or discomfort. All this is normal. We are used to three (large) meals daily, and our bodies have adjusted to this comfortable and enjoyable habit. It takes time and discipline to turn our hunger to worship and prayer. Walk by faith, not feelings.

Sometimes, you will feel as if fasting is worthless and nothing is happening. Focus on the fact that you are obeying God and desire to know Him.

At the same time, be wise and alert to the impact of fasting on your energy levels. Try to avoid doing anything too physically demanding, and end your fast with a light meal. Practically, I've found it essential to set beginning and ending times and stick to them. Also, I usually have some scriptures or a list of prayers to help focus my mind.

In his book 'How To Pray', Pete Grieg shares that the best advice he was given regarding prayer was to *'keep it simple, keep it real, keep it up.'* [9] When the disciples asked Jesus to teach them to pray, he gave them a straightforward prayer. [10] Come to God honestly and regularly and don't feel you must use formal, religious language to communicate. Spend time talking and spend time listening or reading scripture. Prayer and fasting are powerful tools in the journey of spiritual maturity.

Questions

1. Do you have a regular personal devotional time with God? What would you say are the main benefits? What has this chapter offered that might encourage you to persevere or grow in this discipline?

2. If you don't have a personal devotional time at present, how could you start to do so? What would it look like?

- Where would you do it?

- What time of day?

- How long will you spend with God?

- What will you do in the time?

- Are there any incentives to help you look forward to this time?

- What will help you to make this a regular thing?

- Is there anyone you could do this with?

3. Have you ever spent time meditating on scripture? If so, what did you do and what were the benefits? When could you next spend time in the Bible and how would you meditate on it?

4. If you've never meditated on scripture, how might you start? What is there in this chapter that would help or encourage you?

5. What specific situation or person could you start to pray for on a regular basis?

6. Have you ever fasted, or do you fast regularly? If so, how would you say this is of benefit to your spiritual life?

7. If the thought of going without food is daunting or even terrifying, why do you think that is? Are you putting food before God in some way? Is food a difficult or "no-go" area that you need help with, and if so, where might you find the help you need?

8. Could you fast at some point this week? Maybe just miss one meal, and spend the time with God instead.

---

1. Matthew 26; Mark 14, Luke 22:44

2. 21st Century Evangelicals. Time for discipleship. (Evangelical Alliance report. 2014), p16 https://issuu.com/evangelicalalliance/docs/21st_century_evangelicals_-_discipl

3. Jen Wilkin, Don't Expect Instant Gratification from Your 'Quiet Time' Christianity Today, March 21, 2022, www.christianitytoday.com

4. Donald Whitney, Spiritual Disciplines for the Christian Life, (Navpress, 2014), p.28

5. Richard Foster, 'Celebration of Discipline' (HarperOne, 1998 — 3rd Ed.)

6. 1 Corinthians 9:27

7. Jentezen Franklin 'Fasting' (Charisma House, 2008), Chapter 2

8. Richard Foster, 'Crucifying Our Will: Praying Through the Struggle to Let Go', Knowing and Doing Journal, Teaching Quarterly for Discipleship of Heart and Mind, p.1

9. Pete Greig, 'How to Pray- a simple guide for normal people' (John Murray Press, 2019)

10. Matthew 6:9-13

"As the church, we are in community together trying to fulfill this Great Commission that Jesus left us with. As we gently press into each other, we form one united thing, His church. As we work together, sharing the space God gives us to do His work, we all become shaped a little different. We all become a little more like Him."

Jennifer L. Lane
(Faith Adventures: Stories of Learning with an Unseen God)

TWELVE

(IN) RELATIONSHIP WITH OTHERS

L et's turn to the tools God uses within a trusted Christian community (IN). Sadly, I've spoken to many Christians for whom the church family has gone terribly wrong. Our desire to honour our church leaders has sometimes opened a door to narcissism and control, with the result that leaders have misused their authority to manipulate and destroy people's lives. Some church members can experience terrible spiritual trauma and find themselves voiceless and unheard. On the other hand, faith leaders have sometimes become victims of painful witch hunts and accusations and are left with nothing, their reputation in tatters.

These experiences can undermine our willingness to open up to others and embrace vulnerability. It leaves wounds that are difficult to heal, yet however difficult it is to hear, the church community is where God intends us to mature. Author Paul Pettit underlines this vital link between spiritual formation and community. He concludes, *"The goal of my spiritual growth is not my own individual growth apart from the body, but my maturity and development within the body and for the body."*[1] Somehow we need to gently help people regain trust and openness in our church families; otherwise, our growth will be stunted and limited.

Shamebuster

Around ten years ago, I started to notice my own growth had stalled, and I struggled to figure out what was happening. I would sit down with other church leaders to help them talk through their own personal development, but I didn't know who *I* could turn to for help. I spent several years asking God for a mentor, but none was forthcoming, so I contacted a few friends. One immediately said they knew someone who could help me out. I travelled to the United States and met with the head of counselling at a Christian University. Clearly, God knew I needed an expert to help me out of my mess!

I sat beside him with a list of around a dozen issues I knew about. I was just about to talk them all through with him when he interrupted and said, *"Just tell me the one thing you find hardest to tell me about"*. I gulped, immediately knowing which one I didn't want to talk about. It glared at me from my journal, daring me to reveal its secret. I took a deep breath and began to tell him how all my life, I had struggled with my body image, an unhealthy relationship with food, and an overwhelming desire to look a certain way to win acceptance. After a lengthy conversation, we drew out this diagram. It's meant to look like a see-saw or balance beam that pivots at the centre.

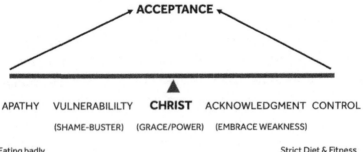

APATHY	VULNERABILILTY	**CHRIST**	ACKNOWLEDGMENT	CONTROL
	(SHAME-BUSTER)	(GRACE/POWER)	(EMBRACE WEAKNESS)	

Eating badly	Strict Diet & Fitness
Feeling fat	Feeling godly
Shame	Pride
Perceived Rejection	Rejection
& judgement	& judgement

It shows my desire for acceptance and the two opposite ways in which I fail to find it. At one end of the seesaw, I lurch towards controlling my diet and exercise to make myself look more acceptable in other people's eyes. Successful dieting and fitness leads to me feeling good about myself and to a sense of godliness, but this stokes my sense of pride and achievement, which ultimately works against my need for God. So I'm ultimately frustrated because, although I'm working hard, I'm feeling even further away from my desired goal of acceptance. The Apostle Peter tells us that God rejects the proud and gives grace to the humble.[2] So even if I'm successful, I end up with rejection.

At other times, I lurch towards the other end of the seesaw for a season, shifting from control to apathy. This is where I eat all the food groups I shouldn't, which leads to me feeling fat and ugly, with a deeper sense of shame. I'm embarrassed about my body and my lack of discipline. Even though I'm living very differently from the other side of the balance beam, I still end up in the same place, feeling rejected by others. This seesaw swing from apathy to control and back again is an unbalanced life that ends with me feeling an even deeper sense of rejection – the very thing I was trying to escape!

My counsellor kindly pointed out that the way through is always turning to Christ. Only in him do I receive grace in my weakness and the power to change. But I needed another factor to be at work - vulnerability. He described it as a shame buster. Slowly, I began to break the power of shame and pride in my life by letting others know about my struggle.

The other important step was acknowledging my problem to myself and embracing it. Instead of pretending or ignoring my issues I needed to admit I had an unhealthy relationship with food, and a negative body image. This involves taking a long, hard look at my weakness and brokenness that both humbles my proud heart and in turn, empowers me to challenge these powerful ingrained coping mechanisms.

As I've shared these painful experiences with other people, I've found that many live like this. Their issue may not be with food, but they lurch from apathy to control as they battle with insecurity, self-control, stress, and anger, without ever really dealing with the issue. It's the age-old battle of legalism and licence.

People spend a huge amount of energy either controlling their behaviours or languishing in apathy or guilt, but they never get to bring the issue entirely to Jesus. Some struggle to open up to others and so the shame multiplies. Or they feel incapable of owning their weakness and so pretend all is well and push their failures down out of sight.

I've found that, like me, many people endure seasons of stagnation followed by seasons of intentional pursuit, only to discover that both methods tend to lead us away from healing. I was using the wrong things to find acceptance. I needed to let others know about my struggles to break the power of shame, and I required grace and strength to change truly.

Talking about it with others, yes, it was humbling but it brought a breakthrough and a renewed desire for holiness. I'd thought I was an open, vulnerable leader, yet I had been hiding the very things I struggled with most. It taught me how shame can be the biggest obstacle to change, as it keeps our issues locked away from sight. God and others cannot access those broken places, and we're left dealing with surface issues and wondering why we're not experiencing transformation. It taught me the importance of finding relational contexts where weakness can be shared and hope for change imparted. This chapter will explore three ways God can use community to bring about our transformation.

1) The Power of Relationships

I recently watched a nature documentary that was both beautiful and brutal. Using a drone, the programme showed an aerial view of a herd of wildebeests on a pilgrimage through an African plain. It was an amazing sight, the synchronised movement, the dust, the speed of thousands of animals, jostling and jumping as they migrated. Their vast numbers gave them protection from the various predators waiting to pick off those separated from the pack.

The camera then followed a pride of lionesses scanning the horizon for their prey. Suddenly they spotted the lone wildebeest they'd been waiting for, a single animal that had become separated from the herd. Its head was down and it was idly feeding, paying little attention to its impending disaster. You know what's coming. The lionesses crept up stealthily and silently, staying low and unseen in the long grass before exploding out to attack the lone animal.

It's a sober lesson for the Christian going it alone. '*Your enemy the devil,*' says Peter, '*prowls around like a roaring lion looking for someone to devour.*' (1 Peter 5:8) In the long run, we can't survive in this brutal world alone, let alone grow more Christlike. We need to live in the pack, in the church family, to flourish on planet Earth. The church community is a God-given ecosystem with huge potential to help us mature.

Lone Christians don't grow. Long-term isolation is not conducive to sanctification, and discipleship at a distance doesn't work. We need proximity to one another for spiritual growth to happen. Formation by information is unhelpful. Sanctification needs to happen with real people in real life; gaining knowledge in books and lectures is not enough. Without people, inner life transformation becomes a self-help project full of blindspots. There is a good reason why professional golfers are helped by golf coaches who are not as good as them. They can't see their own swing. We need community to raise a disciple. Sadly, the internet age means we can forget this and seek out online teaching and worship, which leaves us bloated with information yet experiencing a transformational famine.

Disciples need to avoid solitary Christianity and forgo the crowd to seek out the small and intimate. The New Testament rarely presents a disciple outside of a Spirit-empowered community. In fact, the Apostle Peter seems to think of a Christian as one who is simultaneously joined to Christ and to other living stones in God's new temple (the church).[3] Jesus also does very little one-on-one discipleship. Even when he confronts Peter over his denial, the other disciples are present in the background.

The Apostle Paul emphasises the relational dynamics in discipleship: fathers and mothers with sons and daughters. Notice how he calls Christians to follow his example: '*I am writing this not to shame you but to warn you as my dear children. Even if you had ten thousand guardians in Christ, you do not have many fathers, for in Christ Jesus I became your father through the gospel. Therefore I urge you to imitate me.*' (1 Corinthians 4:14-16) He's a spiritual father speaking to his spiritual children. His favourite term for a Christian is 'brother' or 'sister'. He sets discipleship within a framework of the church family.

Discipleship is something we *are* together

The frequency of the term '*one another*' (fifty-nine times in the New Testament) shows us the emphasis on relational discipleship. A breakdown of those verses shows us 'one anothering' centring around unity (35%), love (35%), humility (15%) and encouragement and edification (15%). This 'one anothering' does not speak to one's individual relationship with God or relationship with oneself, but deals with our life together as a new spiritual family, where we grow together. Discipleship is not only something we *do* to one another but something we *are* together. Everyone, all the time, encourages and contends for one another to follow Jesus.

Last year I spoke with a young man in our church who was struggling with long-term illness. He explained how difficult it was to motivate himself to get involved in church life and our Sunday services. I gently encouraged him to recognise that the lie he must fight was the lie of thinking he should go it alone. He was wrong to think that he was better off at home alone rather than with others. Yes, church members may ask the wrong questions or seek to give unwanted advice for his recovery, but ultimately he would find healing and grace in the body of Christ, not outside of it.

I recently spoke with him about his choices to keep attending services and his small group. He'd realised that self-reliance and isolation don't work in the long run and that instead, God was using the steady consistency of engaging with community each Sunday to work in his life. He had developed patience with well-meaning but difficult people and even found himself praying with those who had similar struggles to his own. His choice to remain in an imperfect family led to greater degree of healing in his life.

As we spend time together, particularly with others different from ourselves, sanctification really kicks in. It's often in difficult communities with difficult people (including ourselves) that we truly mature. These diverse communities are where we practice the gospel together. We confess, repent, forgive, extend grace and learn to love.

People or programmes?

Too often, churches have equated discipleship with programmes or preaching instead of deep, vulnerable friendships. We need these types of more formal training but we should always be biased towards relational discipleship within the church family.

Alicia Britt Chole makes a powerful argument for relationships above programmes: '*Program was far safer, more controllable, and reproducible - less risky, less messy, less intrusive. It seemed easier to give someone an outline than an hour, a well worn book than a window into our humanity. How easy it is to substitute informing people for investing in people, to confuse organising people with actually discipling people. Life is not the offspring of program or paper. Life is the offspring of life. Jesus prioritised shoulder to shoulder mentoring because His prize was much larger than information, it was integration.*'[4]

The quant English idiom '*warp and woof*' comes from the sixteenth century and alludes to the threads that run lengthwise (warp) and crosswise (woof) in a woven fabric. It describes the underlying structure and pattern of something. Discipleship that is the warp and woof of community is the best sort. It thrives when it's found in the ups and downs of life and is naturally part of everyday environments - chatting with passing friends from the front yard, doing the washing up together, watching children play sports, laying the table and enjoying a simple meal.

This sort of relational discipleship means everyone is actively investing in one another rather than having a hierarchical mentoring scheme. It stops people from feeling like a project and promotes mutual learning. Everyone can share responsibility for self-disclosure and an agenda for change. It stops us from thinking that '*one size fits all*' and frees us to treat people as individuals.

Holy Hospitality

In the Western church we have largely forgotten the power of opening our homes and sharing meals. Hospitality doesn't depend on home ownership but is rather a disposition or attitude of making others feel loved, served and at home in our company. It is treating strangers in a way that makes them feel warmly befriended. The New Testament exhorts Christians to embrace this loving posture in order to help those needing shelter and develop generosity of heart.[5]

Hospitality orientates us around the needs of others. It frees us from our preoccupation with ourselves and encourages us to be open and generous and put the needs of others before ourselves. Hospitality is a powerful little fulcrum that can produce a large change in our souls. It is a gift that can grow and develop with practice but shouldn't be confused with entertainment, which is about impressing people with our cooking skills, cleanliness or the size of our house. Hospitality is about service and intentionally opening our hearts, our time and, often, our fridge!

Triplets

Having said discipleship works best in everyday life, we also structure our community life for it at Mosaic. This approach allows new people to have a clear pathway into deeper community. We encourage everyone to be part of a small group and a triplet. The small group (around ten people) provides a context for community, prayer and shared mission. However, people need a smaller group where they can open up about their personal lives. So our triplets are a safe place to grow closer to Jesus, read scripture, share struggles, and do the 'one-anothering' the Bible calls us to.

Triplets are peer-led, though they often work best when at least one of the three has been part of a group before, so that a healthy group has already been modelled to them. Having three people naturally shifts the group from hierarchical (one leader mentoring someone) to relational. It leads to a greater dependence on Jesus rather than the leader. When you have just two people, you can find both are struggling with the same thing, and both end up just as stuck as the other. A third person often brings perspective and can motivate the other two to keep pursuing transformation.

We've also found that triplets only work because of the church's disciple-making culture. Just as farmers use a variety of inputs to make their crops grow (soil preparation, planting seeds, sun, rain, fertiliser, nutrients, and lots of hard work), so disciples need a whole discipleship culture (rather than just an imposed structure) to flourish. Simply starting triplets is unlikely to work in isolation; they need a discipleship 'environment' or 'culture' in order to thrive and grow.

We also occasionally run training to help keep triplets healthy and allow groups to multiply to include new people. We provide sample questions and formats for the groups to use, and triplets also provide a context for follow-up talks from Sundays and support through the various trials of life we face.

Ultimately we want a church where everyone can have deep friendships and can be open and honest about their discipleship challenges. In one sense, we want this to simply be in our culture and everyday life. Triplets provide a structural, intentional way to build this into the life of the church.

2) Confession

The second common means of transformation with others is confession. Author Max Lucado explains, *'Confession is not telling God what he doesn't know. Impossible. Confession is not complaining. If I merely recite my problems and rehash my woes, I'm whining. Confession is not blaming. Pointing fingers at others without pointing any at me feels good, but it doesn't promote healing. Confession is so much more. Confession is a radical reliance on grace. A proclamation of our trust in God's goodness. "What I did was bad," we acknowledge, "but your grace is greater than my sin, so I confess it."*[6]

When we confess, we're simply being honest about our sin and letting the grace of God flow over our mistakes. There is power in embracing this sort of honesty, because we're good at lying to ourselves and justifying our sinful choices.

Confession also exposes the weakness of sin's promises and how embarrassingly unsatisfying it can be. As we confess, we pray that we begin to hate the sin or at least see it as God sees it. We ask that God will unpick some of our excuses and reasoning for indulging in certain sins. It takes courage and confidence in the grace of God.

When King David slept with Bathsheba and then arranged the death of her husband, he had everything to lose and so kept his sin hidden. Psalm 32:2-4 describes his internal battle.

'When I kept silent,
my bones wasted away
through my groaning all day long.
For day and night
your hand was heavy on me;
my strength was sapped
as in the heat of summer.'

Clearly, David was in the wrong, but God did not abandon him. God wanted restoration and fellowship with David, so he sent the prophet Nathan to confront him. Like David, many of us have coping strategies that hide, blame, deny, or excuse sin and we forget that confession to a loving God brings relief and comfort. David was eventually able to declare,

'Blessed is the one
whose transgressions are forgiven,
whose sins are covered.
Blessed is the one
whose sin the Lord does not count against them
and in whose spirit is no deceit.' (Psalm 32:1-2)

Confession to God and then to others is often the moment when we draw a line under a certain sin and stop. It helps us to truly recognise what we have done wrong in a concrete way. It deepens our awareness of the effects of our behaviour and brings us into the light of Christ that brings healing and forgiveness.

A confessing church is one that is humble and reliant on the grace of God. If people are open with each other about their weaknesses then it stops others feeling that they're the only ones failing. Healthy confession deals with the shame we can feel and is powerfully freeing. The resulting sense of restoration that comes after someone has finally admitted their struggles and then basked in the mercy of God is a beautiful thing to witness.

3) Embracing Social and Cultural Diversity

The third (IN) tool that God uses to transform us is when we befriend and serve those who are different from us. The church is built for diversity. A multicultural family is the design and desire of God. Jesus has created one new tribe in Christ, breaking every dividing wall between cultures and peoples. A diverse community is what heaven looks like.

This means our diversity is something to be prized. We should not pretend that everybody is the same, or 'see no colour'. Diversity is good. When we read in Galatians 3:28 that "*There is neither Jew nor Gentile, slave nor free, male nor female*", it cannot mean that the gospel wipes out all human difference. We don't all become race, class and gender neutral. No, it means that the gospel rightly orders our differences, with our identity in Christ being primary. After all, the God in whose image we are made is himself a mysterious unity of eternal difference. The Father is not the Son; the Son is not the Spirit; the Spirit is not the Father; yet they are one. Therefore, our church is called not to be 'colour-blind' but to recognise and celebrate the richness of our God-given differences.

However, Martin Luther King Jr.'s remarks in the New York Times in August 1964 still ring true today, '*We must face the sad fact that at the eleven o'clock hour on Sunday morning when we stand to sing, we stand in the most segregated hour in America.*' Division, segregation and hostility exist among genders, ages, races, families, neighbourhoods, and nations. Diversity becomes disunity. We must face the reality that however lovely or compassionate we may be, we have preferences and prejudices. We fail to love others or we love only those who are similar to us. We make judgments about people. We often unconsciously exclude people. We make people feel ignored, unloved and less than others.

Yet, in Christ, we're now family – brothers and sisters with the same father, and with new responsibilities towards each other. The Apostle Paul says Jesus preaches a double peace - peace with God through grace alone and peace with one another in a new, reconciled body. *"He (Jesus) put to death their hostility,"* (Ephesians 2:16). Healthy churches are meant to be diverse. Our communities should at least reflect the social and cultural diversity of their village, town or city. Within these diverse communities, we are transformed. God uses people different from us to shape us into his likeness.

Peter experienced this personally in Acts 10 and 11. After a vision from God of a sheet filled with unclean animals that he is instructed to kill and eat, Peter realises God wants to reach Gentiles as well as Jews, as he hears God declare, *'Do not call anything impure that God has made clean' (Acts 10:15).* He then accepts the invitation of the Roman centurion Cornelius and goes to his home to share the gospel with him and his household. That scary step across cultural boundaries led to a profound transformation in Peter's heart. He declares to the gathered crowd, *'I now realise how true it is that God does not show favouritism but accepts from every nation the one who fears him and does what is right' (Acts 10:34-35).* Peter receives revelation (Gentile mission is important to God) alongside sanctification (God deals with his narrow-minded prejudice). He experiences a breaking of ground internally as he breaks ground externally.

We're not meant to stay in our lane. Spending time with people who are different from us has the potential to humble us and take us out of our comfort zones. As we build friendships across cultural divides, we learn that other cultures have much to teach us, and we gain a greater understanding of the struggles and opportunities faced by people who are wealthier or poorer than us.

And as different cultures bump up against each other, we are forced to practise forgiveness and reconciliation. We are forced to confront our prejudices and stereotyping and transition from tolerance to genuine love. We move beyond our native culture to a kingdom culture of love and acceptance.

My small mid-week group at Mosaic has people from America, Zimbabwe, Portugal, Nigeria and Kenya. We have white and black British people from working-class and middle-class backgrounds. We have children under three and adults in their sixties. This wonderfully diverse concoction of people means we have to work hard to get along. Our many misunderstandings mean we must keep forgiving and thinking the best of one another. We must spend time listening to one another in order to truly understand and empathise. Curiosity will encourage us to learn about different values and traditions and we compromise on our own preferences in order to honour one another. All this moves us from self-serving consumerism to other-centred family.

If we feel comfortable and unchallenged in all our friendships, we may need to seek out some friends who are not like us. The church is meant to be a place where people who are very different from one another, yet united in Christ, learn to love one another. Time with people from other cultures and backgrounds will expose any pride or self-importance. We will have to decide whether we're willing to listen to and learn from people who do things differently from us. We'll eat unfamiliar food and face different parenting styles. We'll see how other cultures worship, pray and study the Bible. We'll all turn up to the meeting at different times and have no idea when it will end. All of which, if we let it, helps us to become unpretentious, generous-hearted people.

Questions

1. In what ways do you practise hospitality? How could you grow in this gift? Who could you befriend and serve? Are there any individuals in your life who need someone to welcome them into family?

2. Think of the people in your small group or church community or wider social circles. How different are they from you in terms of age, class, ethnicity, gender? What are some of the lessons you are learning

from growing closer to people who are not like you? How are you celebrating your diversity? How are you dealing with areas of friction?

3. Are there one or two other people in your church community who share your desire to grow? Could you reach out to them and start reading this book together?

For a free PDF of 'A guide to Triplets' visit www.matthatch.org

---

1. Paul Pettit, ed., 'Foundations of Spiritual Formation: A Community Approach to Becoming Like Jesus' (Grand Rapids, MI: Kregel Publications, 2008), p.271

2. 1 Peter 5:5

3. 1 Peter 2:4-5

4. Alicia Britt Chole, 'Purposeful Proximity - Jesus' model of mentoring' Enrichment Journal: A Journal of Pentecostal Ministry (Spring 2001) quoted in Greg Ogden, 'Transforming Discipleship', (Intervarsity Press 2003), p. 125

5. 1 Peter 4:8-9; Hebrews 13:1-2; 1 Timothy 5:10

6. Max Lucado, Grace: More than we Deserve, Greater than we Imagine, Thomas Nelson. Quoted in The Pastors Workshop www.thepastorswor kshop.com/sermon-quotes-on-confession-of-sin/

"The mission of Jesus is yours to participate in. It has always been God's intention to choose normal, everyday people, and to show his amazing power and glory through them. He's not looking for the most impressive person because he already is that person."

Jeff Vanderstelt
(Saturate: Being Disciples of Jesus in the Everyday Stuff of Life)

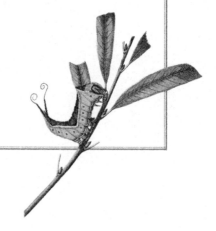

THIRTEEN

(OUT) RELATIONSHIP WITH THE WORLD

A fter looking at the biblical tools of transformation in our relationship with God (UP) and others (IN), we move towards the tools God uses as we spend time with those who don't know Jesus yet (OUT).

1) Local and Global Mission

Engaging in mission transforms us. Maturity happens as we move towards the lost. We simply can't be mature disciples without also being evangelistic. Colin Marshall and Tony Payne, authors of the classic discipleship book, 'The Trellis and the Vine', suggest '*The Christian without a missionary heart is an anomaly*[1].' Sadly, a missional lifestyle is often seen as an optional extra. Christians can see themselves as *either* discipleship-focused or mission-focused, yet they're meant to go hand in hand.

Evangelism and discipleship may seem to conflict because they seem to have an order. Many of us feel we can't engage in witnessing until God has matured us. We believe we need a long preparation time before we're unleashed on the world. We get sorted first, and then we do mission. Yet Jesus clearly didn't perceive discipleship and evangelism this way. When Jesus sent out his disciples with authority to preach the gospel, heal the sick and cast out demons, they were far from the finished article. They had to learn on the job. Jesus gave them feedback, and they matured *in* the mission, not before it. Hence the Great Commission is better translated, '*As you are going, make disciples.*'[2] The going is assumed and expected, and maturity and multiplication are meant to happen along the way.

The early church saw itself as a missionary movement.[3] Everyone was included in God's plan for the gospel to go to the ends of the earth. Early Christians stood on the shoulders of the patriarchs who believed God had blessed them so that they in turn would be a blessing to the whole earth. They embraced the mandate to build the church and preach the gospel to every people group. If you like, there was a strong, powerful river flowing to the nations, and if they didn't engage in this global mission but reached out only to their own locality, it was like damming the river. It might create a pleasant reservoir, but it would leave the nations in drought.

How does this relate to discipleship? If we make spiritual formation an end in itself, we've missed an essential aspect of our calling. Remember, discipleship is 'the work of becoming like Christ *and* embracing his mission'. The focus of discipleship is for the sake of others.

As Dallas Willard, (who is probably one of the most influential modern writers on discipleship), says, '*The Church is for discipleship and discipleship is for the world.*'[4] They shouldn't be separated; one cannot be done without the other. God works *in* his disciples in order to work *through* his disciples. Mission and maturity are interwoven and reciprocal. Author Robert Mulholland Jr., who has written extensively on Christian formation, agrees, '*No healthy spiritual formation is possible apart from mission with Christ. Similarly, no transformative mission with Christ is possible apart from formation in Christ.*'[5] The goal is always loving God and loving others, both locally and globally.

Maturity is understanding your role in God's mission

Movement leader David Devenish[6] has spent his life calling people to the mission of God. He states, *'All of God's plans have been fulfilled in Christ. Through his suffering on the cross and his resurrection, he brought into effect the rule of God and the blessing of every nation, uniting believers from every nation himself. Christ is now at work in us believers from many nations by his Spirit, who is the hope and guarantee of his new creation purposes....Christ has fulfilled all God's purposes; I am in Christ, he is in me, and so I have a part in the fulfilment of God's mighty plan.'*

David explains that too often we get caught up in the benefits of our faith for us and us alone. We love the peace, joy and forgiveness, but our individualistic mindset means we tend to think of our sanctification as a private exercise that involves just 'myself and God', whereas true maturity is found in understanding our involvement in the big, biblical story of God's work in the world. His ultimate purpose is to bring everything in heaven and earth together under the rule of Christ and our level of engagement with this will determine the level of our maturity. Transformation happens as we expand our gaze to find our place and involvement in God's mission.

Local Mission

We are sent, as Jesus was sent, to share the good news of Jesus with everyone we know. As we endeavour to witness to friends and family, we will find several things happening. We will probably find many people are not interested in discovering Jesus for themselves. They may seem closed to our apologetics or our gentle and winsome explainations of our faith. This can be intensely disappointing. It's hard to keep in faith for the transformation of people with whom we've spent years sharing the gospel, apparently without success.

We can also feel frustrated at our efforts and failures to represent Christ to the people who know us best. Our family may still revert in their minds to the old, outdated version of ourselves they knew from our younger years. This means they cannot properly hear our story or take us seriously. Many of us can feel under the spotlight and judged for any actions or decisions that may be viewed by them as 'un-Christian'. Family can be quick to point out our faults and ignore the internal transformation that God has done.

This humbling experience can break any pride or over-confidence in our own ability and can shift our dependence towards God. It has the potential to harden our hearts and soften our resolve to pray for those close to us or it can make us more desperate than ever to see change in their lives. Personally, I find I can fluctuate between these two ends of the spectrum and I regularly need to repent and ask God to help me trust him for breakthrough in local mission among friends and family.

Cross-cultural mission

Anyone who has engaged in evangelism, especially cross-culturally, understands how difficult it is. This can lead us towards deeper humility and teachability. Bible teacher and church planter Andy McCullough links cross-cultural mission to Jesus' parable of the seed that dies in order to multiply. He says, *'When you enter a new culture it can feel like death (if you do it well!)...You go from being competent and successful in your home culture to dependent and babyish in the new. You go from being able to express yourself to utter inarticulacy. You go from being respected to being misunderstood and unable to defend yourself. You go from feeling 'useful' to God to feeling the total opposite. It's like dying! Dying to what you knew, dying to the right to comment, dying to things that you had assumed to be absolutes. It hurts.*[7]

Cross-cultural mission involves us dying to self-sufficiency, where our best efforts and arguments may not be as effective as they were in our own culture. We may have to learn a new language and new customs; even reaching the nations in our home towns and cities in the UK, requires us to listen, learn and serve before we have the right, or indeed the ability, to share the gospel message. And the process of engaging with people from different cultures and learning from them will teach us a great deal, and help us to walk humbly among those we are trying to reach. Wonderfully, Jesus' parable reminds us that if a seed (us) is buried properly it will take root, grow, and in time multiply into something greater. God loves to resurrect life out of the ashes of surrender and service.

In the last few decades, cross-cultural mission has taken on something of a new perspective, as the western church has found itself benefiting from the prayers and expertise of the church in the global south, where Christianity is growing exponentially. Whereas in the past, the pattern was for western missionaries to go to the global south with the gospel, those churches now have a great deal to offer the West in terms of their theological understanding of mission and the practical ways they can help us engage in evangelism. We need their faith, expectation, and commitment to prayer. We have much to learn from their attitude to suffering for Christ and their willingness to be that seed that dies in order to multiply. This reversal of the historical direction of travel of the gospel challenges any prejudices we might have held about our own western cultural or missional superiority and fuels our hope for many to be saved.

They will see our good works

Sanctification is a necessary part of evangelism, because people *see* our lives more than they listen to our words. It seems the early church embraced a lifestyle of provocative witness. The Apostle Peter instructed his churches, *'Live such good lives among the pagans that, though they accuse you of doing wrong, they may see your good deeds and glorify God on the day he visits us.'* (1 Peter 2:12) The Christian author Frank Laubach summarises it nicely, *'The simple program of Christ for winning the whole world is to make each person He touches magnetic enough with love to draw others.* [8]

Accounts from early historians indicate that many pagans were converted by seeing how Christians lived. In the third century, Eusebius (quoting Bishop Dionysius of Alexandria) described a terrible and unexpected plague in his city and observed the Christians' response; *'Most of our brother-Christians showed unbounded loved and loyalty, never sparing themselves and thinking only of one another. Heedless of the danger, they took charge of the sick, attending to their every need and ministering to them in Christ, and with them departed this life serenely happy; for they were infected by others with the disease, drawing on themselves the sickness of their neighbours and cheerfully accepting their pains.* [9] Eusebius goes on to state that because of their compassion in the midst of the plague, the Christians' *'deeds were on everyone's lips, and they glorified the God of the Christians.'* Can you see the mutuality - engaging in mission can lead to transformation, and transformation empowers our mission.

How to engage in mission?

How do we move towards this? Much has been written about being a church on mission. It involves more than just evangelistic activities or church programmes; it means having people constantly announcing and demonstrating God's kingdom.

However, studies suggest it takes only five years for a new Christian to lose all their unchurched friends, and many in the church find solace in solitude and withdrawal from the world. The result is that many of us are not prepared to share our faith or the gospel message with those who don't know Jesus.

Some of the lessons we've learnt at Mosaic consist of helping people change their expectations and readiness to share the gospel as the sent people of God. We want to ensure that everyone has tools for sharing their testimony or explaining the gospel. And we want to deal with fear of rejection so that we feel able to be open about our faith and not hide it. [10]

We also try to help our church members identify their gifts, talents and passions. We offer training in how to do Bible studies with non-Christians. We encourage our small groups (called mission groups) to understand the context and needs of their community.

While we're aware of the ethical and environmental concerns surrounding short-term mission, we've found that short-term cross-cultural missions (which can be local and not involve much travel or expense) supercharge discipleship. I'm not advocating Christian tourism or any lack of sensitivity to the impact of a trip on local believers. Yet moving beyond our own neighbourhood expands our love for others. It helps us see that we are broken vessels who need the power of God and his gospel to truly see transformation. It makes us pray and depend on God. It gives us a fresh boldness and faith that can be taken home with us.

Building a church of Mission *and* Discipleship

We've tried to structure our church in a way that it pushes people out into the world. Our small group system is organised around mission: you join a group because you want to reach specific people or places together. The idea is to push against the 'gravitational force' most churches experience, by which people tend to gravitate away from non-Christians and into the church family.

For the last fifteen years, we've hosted an annual conference called LOVE:NATIONS to help people engage with local and global mission. It's a small part of a wider plan to move our congregation into the world. We want everyone to figure out their role in reaching the nations abroad or on their doorstep. When people are convinced about their missional role, it motivates them to deeper surrender, encounter and obedience. They become aware of their failings and fragility and need for Jesus much more than when they are nestled safely in the comforts of the Christian community. It stops us Western Christians thinking we are at the centre of the Christian world. It humbles us. It connects us to the heart of God. It helps us suffer with those that are persecuted for their faith. In sum, a church alive to global mission will be a church alive to disciple-making.

2) Working with the Marginalised

I'm not sure if I fully understand this dynamic, but the scriptures connect my healing and growth with serving the most vulnerable in society. Social justice and transformation go hand in hand.

Isaiah famously declares the type of fasting God is looking for: *'Is not this the kind of fasting I have chosen: to loose the chains of injustice and untie the cords of the yoke, to set the oppressed free and break every yoke? Is it not to share your food with the hungry and to provide the poor wanderer with shelter –when you see the naked, to clothe them, and not to turn away from your own flesh and blood? Then your light will break forth like the dawn, and your healing will quickly appear; then your righteousness will go before you, and the glory of the Lord will be your rear guard. Then you will call, and the Lord will answer; you will cry for help, and he will say: here am I.'* (Isaiah 58:6-9)

Isaiah says we must choose a lifestyle of prioritising marginalised, disadvantaged and vulnerable people. Whether we give, pray or go to the poor, God uses this dynamic to make us more like him. Isaiah prophesies that 'our light will break forth like the dawn' and 'our healing will quickly appear' as we hunger and thirst for justice. Social action is part of our worship and imitation of Jesus.

Perhaps you've watched those TV shows where rebellious children are sent to live with different parents for a week to 'fix' their behavioural problems. The new parents instil new routines and rules. They are consistent and proportional with discipline. They prioritise time together. They eat dinner at the same table. They provide a home that is safe and secure. All the while, the teenager is ignoring them and doing their best to justify their misbehaviour. They constantly complain about the rules and rebel against the love on offer. It's like they're unable to break out of their self-centeredness and personal issues.

And then, near the end of their stay, they are taken to serve the poor and marginalised. Maybe it's a neighbourhood project in the inner city. Or a charity working with children with cancer in the local hospital. Suddenly these rebellious children are face to face with real suffering. They see true pain, grief, or poverty, which somehow makes them come to their senses. They quickly realise their problems pale into insignificance compared with the person in front of them. It humbles them. And suddenly, they are willing to respond positively to their parents and carers.

Your heart becomes bigger

God seems to use a similar process when we serve the underprivileged and work for social justice. Getting closer to hardship helps us come face to face with the person *behind* the need and gives us an understanding of the challenges they face. This can soften our judgement and preconceptions about their situation and life choices or educate us about the injustice many people face.

Compassion is the response of love to suffering. The root of the word in Latin is a compound of *'com'* (with) and *'passio'* (suffer), which gives us the meaning *'to suffer with'*. Compassion is entering into the pain of another. It is feeling someone else's suffering—experiencing it, sharing it, tasting it. It is identifying with the individual and being in solidarity with the sufferer. True compassion is a powerful motivation to move us to action. Compassionate people are intimately connected to God's love for the downtrodden and demeaned, leading them to imitate Jesus' love for the least, last and the lost.

As we learn to love those around us, God breaks our self-sufficiency. He pours out compassion. He gives perspective. He calls out gratitude. He humbles us so that we realise we have more to learn than teach, and more to receive than give. He shows us that the world is much bigger and needier than our own little life. He shares his loving kindness and mercy with us and our love for others increases. He reveals where we can use our resources better and make sacrifices to share what we have. We become passionate about justice issues that reflect the heart of God. We find ourselves growing in appreciation of the blessing in our own lives while learning to place other people's needs on par with ours. Proximity to the poor gives us much more than we can give out.

I remember my wife, Philippa spending time with a homeless man when she was managing a night shelter. Michael had been a train driver until someone had committed suicide by stepping out in front of his train. The trauma of the incident had led to him losing his job, home, family, and eventually, his mind. He now lived in a homemade tent just outside the town but regularly came to stay at the night shelter to be fed, cleaned and patched up. The dirt was ingrained in his skin. He was unkempt and smelled of sweat and urine.

Yet Philippa loved this man, though it hadn't been an easy journey for her. She had lost her own father to suicide when she was eighteen. Her father had been mentally unstable for a long time and lived in seclusion. While Michael was dishevelled and unkempt, she felt God say to love him as she would have wanted her father to be loved if he had become homeless. She found new depths of compassion in serving one of the most vulnerable men in town. God had used Philippa to care for Michael but at the same time, God had sent Michael to make Philippa more like Jesus.

Caution

While serving the underprivileged can lead to greater transformation in our own lives, we must be careful when we start to disciple those we're serving. Natalie Williams and Paul Brown helpfully point out the pitfalls of middle class people discipling the working class or the underprivileged. They warn of imposing external values such as giving up smoking, drinking and gambling while ignoring their own socially acceptable middle-class sins such as gluttony, lying, envy and slander.[11]

Many middle-class people want to send their children to the highest-achieving schools or live in the nicest neighbourhood. They aspire to homeownership as opposed to renting. They want to save for the future rather than spend money while they have it. Yet Jesus didn't teach us these things. While they may be sensible and a good form of stewardship, they are not biblical values to be imposed on others.

Jesus had much to say about the perils of externalism (changing outward behaviour to conform to religious expectations), and a humble and thoughtful posture is needed. Williams and Brown advise us to focus more on love, prayer, encouragement and pursuing Jesus together. In time, the Holy Spirit will start to convict people of their sin rather than well-meaning people pointing out to them what they should or shouldn't do. It is not that we can never challenge people - rather, the point is to double-check that we're not imposing our own cultural external values on people and making them look like us rather than like Jesus.

Serving those on the margins will look different for each of us, yet it's an important component of maturity. I enjoyed discipling a godly church leader who wanted to keep actively serving those in need. He was very busy but had carved out a few hours each week to volunteer at a local food bank. After a while, he confessed that the work was frustrating, slow and thankless. He struggled with the lack of change in the lives of those he visited and frequently questioned whether or not this was a good use of his time. In fact, rather than growing in compassion, he found his heart becoming harder to those in need and society in general. In one sense, he felt he was becoming more ungodly and judgemental.

Bravely he shared his feelings with our discipleship group and we encouraged him to let God use this moment to speak to him. He realised that God wanted to use the powerlessness he felt. Working with the underprivileged wasn't a task to succeed in or a goal to achieve. God wanted to use the sense of impotency to provoke him to new levels of prayerful dependency. He sensed God's grace to him over his lack of love and discovered fresh motivation to persevere in this task. His work with the disadvantaged wasn't outwardly 'successful' but it was inwardly transformational.

Questions

1. What has been your experience of witnessing through your deeds and words to the people in your life? What are some of the discipleship moments you've encountered as you've done this?

2. What next steps could you take to grow in missional living? Are there people around you that God wants you to reach out to in love and service? What things might need to change for this to happen more regularly? Where do you feel 'out of your depth' and in need of God to bring breakthrough?

3. Are there any bridges you could build towards those from a different cultural background to you?

4. What does it look like for you to engage with serving those on the margins of society? What are some of the prejudices that God might want to change in your attitude to the underprivileged?

5. How is God using the marginalised to speak to you and challenge you?

---

1. Colin Marshall and Tony Payne, 'The Trellis and the Vine' (Matthias Media, 2021), p.52

2. Matthew 28:18-20

3. Historian Philip Schaff paints a vivid picture for us: 'It is a remarkable fact that after the days of the Apostles no names of great missionaries are mentioned til the opening of the middle ages...There were no missionary societies, no missionary institutions, no organised efforts in the ante-Nicene age; and yet is less than 300 years from the death of St John the whole population of the Roman empire which was then represented the civilised world was nominally Christianised...And while there were no professional missionaries devoted their whole life to this specific work, every congregation was a missionary society, and every Christian believer a missionary, inflamed by the love of Christ to convert his fellow-men.' - Philip Schaff, History of the Christian Church, 8 vols. (Peabody: Hendrickson, 2006). loc. 12380 quoted in Damian Gerke, In the Way: Church as we know it can be a discipleship movement (again), Network211, Springfield, MO, p.43

4. Dallas Willard, 'How the Disciplines Relate to the Person and Transformation' Talk given October 15, 2010. Found at https://conversatio.org/how-the-disciplines-relate-to-the-person-and-transformation/

5. Robert Mulholland as cited in Nathan A. Finn and Keith Whitfield, eds., Spirituality for the Sent: Casting a New Vision for the Missional Church (Downers Grove, IL: InterVarsity Press, 2017), p 173

6. David Devenish 'Fathering Leaders, Motivating Mission', (Authentic Media, 2011) pp. 264-265

7. Andy McCullough 'Sown' Web Article, April 26, 2023. https://www.unreached.network/sown/

8. Frank Laubach, Man of Prayer (Syracuse, N.Y.: Laubach Literacy International, 1990), page 154.

9. Eusebius, The History of the Church, trans. G. A. Williamson (Harmondsworth: Penguin, 1984), 7.22, 305.

10. John 20:21

11. Natalie Williams and Paul Brown 'Invisible Divides -Class, culture and barriers to belonging in the church' (SPCK, 2022) pp. 32-39

"I can only hope and pray that a century from now (if Christ has not returned) when church historians study the time in which we live that it will be called an age of discipleship."

Daniel Ogden
(Discipleship Essentials)

FOURTEEN

YOU'RE READY TO START

Around five years ago, I found myself struggling emotionally. Even though I loved my job, my church, and my team, I felt dull and lethargic. I found myself retreating from social situations and needing more energy than usual to lead. My internal drive and motivation were fading, and I could feel apathy creeping into my life.

Scottish counsellor and pastor David Murray[1] compares the upkeep of our spiritual life to owning a car. Just as our cars need to be regularly refuelled, re-tuned and repaired, so our souls need proper steps to stay up and running. Many people are overwhelmed, tired, spent, anxious and joyless. Even though they fill their time with good things, their pace is only sustainable if they get regular rest, readjustment and recalibration. Repeatedly ignoring the warning lights on the dashboard ends up in a breakdown. My emotional tiredness was a blinking orange light on my dashboard, telling me to pull over, open the bonnet and take a good look at what needed repairing. Mosaic kindly offered me three months' sabbatical to get the help I needed.

Painfully, during my sabbatical, I found God speaking to me through these verses from Philippians 3:7-8 *'But whatever were gains to me I now consider loss for the sake of Christ. What is more, I consider everything a loss because of the surpassing worth of knowing Christ Jesus my Lord, for whose sake I have lost all things.'* God was asking me to freshly surrender my life to gain Christ.

In truth, it felt hard to hear, given how weak I felt. But a closer look made me realise I had developed a creeping sense of resistance to God and his lordship over my life. This compromise in the little, unseen things meant I was not at peace. I was out of step with the Holy Spirit. I was leading from a place of quiet rebellion and it was killing my passion and joy in God. My engine, so to speak, needed some fine-tuning. This involved repenting and offering my body and soul as a living sacrifice, holy and pleasing to God as my true and proper worship.[2]

I spent a month doing the following. Every day, I'd try to go through another aspect of my life and bring it to God. My comfort, my freedom, my vision, my goals, my dreams, my way of doing things, in sum, my whole life. As I stopped fighting against God, I found fresh motivation and capacity to continue to lead and serve.

All of us will experience these seasons of reflection and personal renewal. The ebb and flow of our faith means there will be times when God comes close and invites us to step deeper into his purposes for our lives. I hope reading this book has led you to a point of decision where you want to move towards the transformation you long for. We've learnt that true and lasting transformation does not come from self-driven, do-your-best externalism. We change by God empowering us by his Spirit as we embrace our true God-given identity.

Remember God's desire for us is a wholesale transformation of the heart that, in turn, impacts our desires and actions. This work of sanctification is central to Jesus' plans for everyone in the church. Look at how the Apostle Paul explains this dynamic. He encourages husbands to look at Christ's self-giving sacrifice for his bride, the church. Jesus' goal is to sanctify her, and present her in radiant beauty and spotless purity. He wants the new creation to be drawn down into the present so that the church would be spotless, with all blemishes, sins and stains removed.[3] Jesus *will* purify us, His church.

This means, despite how we may feel about our transformation, God has determined to complete his work in us. He wants the beauty of the church to be seen by all. He wants our co-operation. Our destiny is glorification but our day-to-day journey is sanctification.

My hope is that this book propels us towards greater surrender, encounter and obedience to Jesus. This can happen in powerful, mountain-top moments but generally, it's a daily commitment to ask God to grow these qualities in our lives.

Practically, we learnt in chapters 6 and 7 about telling our stories and how the past impacts our present. We unpacked the change circle and how we can respond when discipleship moments happen.

Engaging in the spiritual disciplines will help bring us into the presence of God - and wonderfully, the Holy Spirit is very good at forming us into his image and leading us out into his mission. However, there needs to be intention, effort and focus. We learnt in chapter 9 to imagine the person God is making us to be and to carefully pick spiritual disciplines that shape us into that increasingly mature person.

We also spent time looking at some of the tools of transformation focused on UP, IN and OUT. It might be good to imagine these activities as foundational building blocks upon which all the rest of our life is built on.

Just do something

When Jesus tells the parable of the talents[4], encouraging disciples to be faithful with the opportunities and abilities he has given us, he speaks to those of us who feel overwhelmed with life and don't want to mess things up. We can end up thinking we're going to disappoint God, so we play it safe and generally feel miserable.

However, I believe all Christians can live a life hearing God say *'well done good and faithful servant'* simply by investing our talents faithfully. In reality, Jesus doesn't burden us with an impossible task, rather he warns us to avoid doing nothing.

Anyone who embraces these activities will be positioning themselves for transformation. Start small and try to grow consistency. Think of a slow-moving river cutting its way through rock. It's not just its power but its unrelenting persistence that helps it carve its path to the sea. Bit by bit, we move towards maturity. And we can expect transformation to happen. God loves setting people free. Pursuing Christlikeness is like swimming with the tide. God's commitment to our growth should not be underestimated.

The scholar Tom Wright asks the most important question about our purpose in life. *'What are we here for in the first place? The fundamental answer…is that what we're "here for" is to become genuine human beings, reflecting the God in whose image we're made, and doing so in worship on the one hand and in mission, it's full and large sense, on the other; and that we do this not least by "following Jesus". The way this works out is that it produces, through the work of the Holy Spirit, a transformation of character.* [5]

This ultimate question that Wright asks, *'What are we here for?'* should stop us in our tracks. It should apprehend us and shake us from our spiritual slumber. Why am I here and not in heaven? Why has God left me on earth after becoming a Christian? Simply this: God is reforming me into an image bearer with great potential to be transformed into Christ's likeness through worship and mission. He's renewing me from the inside out to join his redemptive story being worked out among all peoples. Let's give ourselves to this magnificent task.

Questions

1. What transformational tools will help you move forward into experiencing change?

2. What happens tomorrow? What is your next move to embrace the transformation you long for?

3. Can you find someone else to share your learning from this book? Sometimes writing it down or verbalising it helps crystalise what God is revealing to you.

1. David Murray, 'Reset - living a Grace-paced life in a burnout culture' (Crossway Books, 2017)

2. Romans 12:1

3. Ephesians 5:26-27

4. Matthew 25:14-30

5. N. T. Wright 'After you believe: Why Christian Character matters' (San Franscisco:HarperOne, 2012), p.26

For free discipleship resources and downloads, visit
www.matthatch.org

This includes an exclusive training video -
*'Three things holding back your transformation and
what you can do about them'*, downloadable PDFs,
and a 'How to start a Triplet' manual.

Printed in Great Britain
by Amazon

37478296R00126